A NEW VIEW

COLLEGE ENGLISH LESSONS FROM AROUND THE WORLD

Myeong-Hee Seong

Lyle A. Lewin

Yoon-Hee Shin

지식인

Authors

Myeong-Hee Seong
Ph.D. in English Education, Korea Univ.
Professor, Eulji University

Lyle A. Lewin
M.A. in Business Administration, Washington State Univ.
Professor, Eulji University

Yoon-Hee Shin
M.A. in English Education
California State University, Fullerton

A New View

College English Lessons From Around The World

2016년 7월 15일 초판 1쇄 발행
2022년 8월 25일 초판 5쇄 발행

지은이 | Myeong-Hee Seong · Lyle A. Lewin · Yoon-Hee Shin
펴낸이 | 김종욱 · 명사동
펴낸곳 | 지식인
등 록 | 제301-2013-134호
주 소 | 서울시 도봉구 도봉로 180길 20 투웨니퍼스트 102동 602호
전 화 | 02)2266-8606 (대)
팩 스 | 02)2266-8607
E-mail | jisikin2013@naver.com
홈페이지 | www.jisikinbook.co.kr

ISBN 978-89-98591-75-5 (93740)

값 14,000원

A New View

College English Lessons From Around The World

Table of Contents

UNIT 01

Speak So That People Want to Listen

What Do You Think?

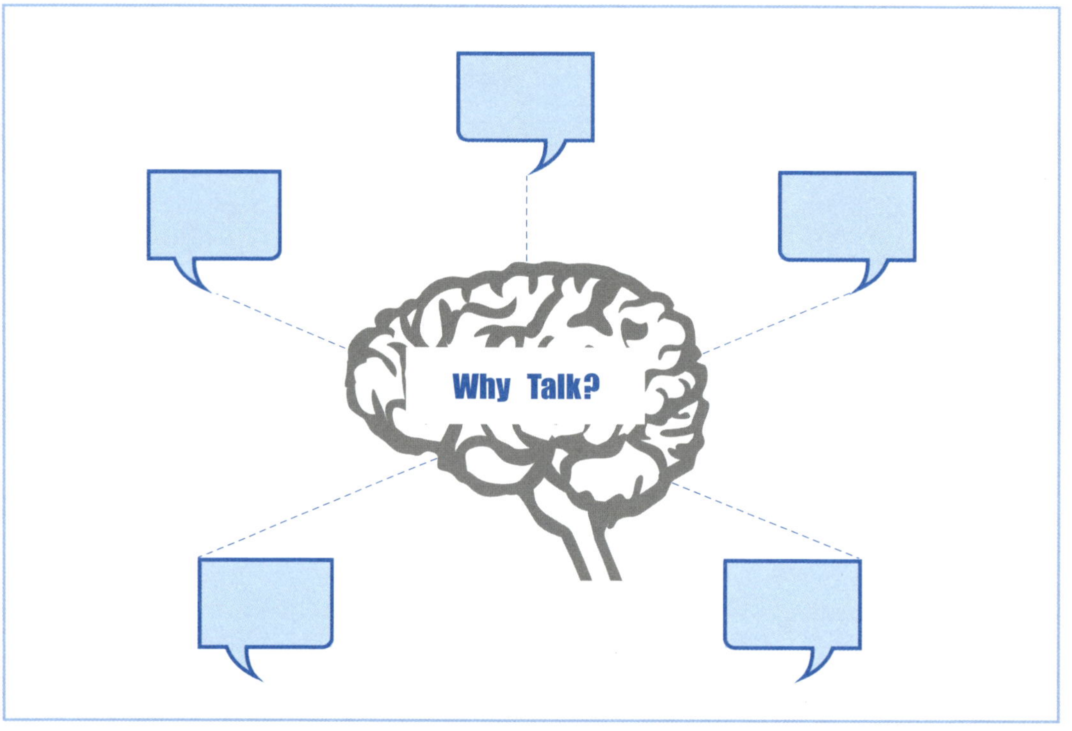

What If?

1. What if you knew someone was lying to you? What would you do?

____

____

____

2. What if you really wanted someone to listen to you? How would you get them to listen closely?

____

____

____

VOCABULARY PREVIEW

1. Read and match the words or phrases with the right meaning.

a. instrument	a. expressing denial or refusal
b. negativity	b. base; something essential
c. excuse	c. genuineness
d. exaggeration	d. quality of being honest and morally upright
e. cornerstone	e. implement or apparatus
f. authenticity	f. an overstatement
g. integrity	g. providing a reason or explanation for release from an obligation

2. Complete the sentences using the words or phrases above.

a. There's a considerable ______________ in his findings. I don't believe him.

b. Which musical ______________ can you play?

c. Late again! Don't make another ______________.

d. The opposite concept of ______________ is positivity.

e. The ______________ of the document could not be proven.

f. The right to privacy is a ______________ of a democratic society.

g. He is reputed to be a man of ______________.

Speak So That People Want to Listen

Adapted from: Julian Treasure

The human voice: It's the instrument we all play. It's probably the most powerful sound in the world. It's the only one that can start a war or say "I love you." And yet many people have a similar experience when they speak, people don't listen to them. Why is that? How can we speak powerfully to make change in the world?

There are six common bad habits that we need to change. The first is gossiping, which is speaking rudely about somebody who's not around. This is not a nice habit, and we know that the person gossiping will probably be gossiping about us five minutes later. Second, is judging. It's very hard to listen to somebody if you know that you're being judged.

The third habit is negativity. For example, at the end of my mother's life, she became very negative and it became hard to listen to her. I remember one day I said to her, "It's October 1 today," and she said, "Yes, isn't that terrible?" Dealing with someone like that takes a lot of energy and it can become very difficult.

The fourth bad habit is making excuses. We've all met someone like that. Maybe we've been that person. Some people just pass problems on to others and don't take responsibility for their actions. Again, it's hard to listen to somebody who is being like that.

Fifth is exaggeration. This means saying things are more than they really are. For example, saying something is great, when it's really just okay. This makes our language less valuable. Exaggeration becomes lying, and we don't want to listen to people we know are lying to us.

The final habit is dogmatism or confusing facts with opinions. When those two things get mixed, you're listening to the wind. If somebody is always telling you their opinions as if they are true, it becomes tough to take that person seriously, and we eventually stop listening.

While those things are negative, I'd like to suggest that there are four really powerful ways that can help our speech become stronger and help us to make changes in the world. Fortunately, these characteristics spell a word. The word is "HAIL."

- H is for honesty. This means being true in what you say.
- A is for authenticity. This means just being yourself.
- I is for integrity. This means actually doing what you say, and being somebody people can trust.
- L is for love.

For love, I don't mean romantic love, but I do mean wishing people well. If we can partner honesty with love, this becomes a great thing. If you're really wishing somebody well, it's hard to judge them at the same time. So, if you want others to really listen: HAIL.

READING COMPREHENSION

【A】*Answer the following questions related to the article.*

1. What is the instrument we can all play?
   a. Piano
   b. Voice
   c. Guitar

2. What type of speaking becomes lying?
   a. Negativity
   b. Exaggeration
   c. Gossip

3. Which of the six bad habits makes our language less valuable?
   a. Negativity
   b. Dogmatism
   c. Exaggeration

4. Always keeping your promises:
   a. Friendly
   b. Integrity
   c. Lonesome

5. Which of the following is not used to make our language more powerful?
   a. Authenticity
   b. Honesty
   c. Strength

[B] *Answer the questions below with a complete sentence.*

1. Why do you think people exaggerate?

____

2. Why is it important to be honest?

____

[C] *Read the following statements about the article. Answer true or false.*

1. The human voice can start a war. [T] / [F]

2. Sometimes when people speak, others don't listen. [T] / [F]

3. Some people don't take responsibility for their actions. [T] / [F]

4. Dogmatism is the same as being negative. [T] / [F]

5. We like to listen to people who are lying. [T] / [F]

[D] *Fill in the following summary with words from the word bank.*

There are seven common bad ❶ ______________ that we need to change if we want people to listen. First, is gossip, which means speaking ❷ ______________ about somebody who's not around. Second, is judging. It's very hard to ❸ ______________ to somebody if you know that you're being judged. The third ❹ ______________ is negativity, and always saying ❺ ______________ things. Next, are ❻ ______________, which means refusing to take responsibility for your actions. The sixth bad habit is exaggeration, which means that we say things are more ❼ ______________ than they really are. The final bad habit is ❽ ______________. This is when people talk about opinions as if they are facts.

Word Bank

habits	negative	important	dogmatism
excuses	listen	characteristic	badly

GRAMMAR BUILDER (Nouns/Articles)

Complete the following paragraphs using the words in parentheses. Change the form of the words if needed.

Practice 1

______________________ will give ______________________ to
(Seoul Metropolitan Government) (identification number)
artworks in its possession as part of its efforts to manage them better. The municipality announced on Friday that 400 of its important ______________ such as monuments
(artwork)
and statutes, will have plaques with their identification ______________, names,
(number)
brief descriptions and management bodies by the end of September. Among them, 81 artworks will be managed by art experts from ______________________,
(city government)
while the rest of them will be managed by public organizations.

Practice 2

Chinese ______________ are a new target for Korea's tourism industry, as they offer
(company)
incentive tours for their high-performance employees. As ______________ tourists
(number of)
reaches up to several thousand at once, more and more provincial governments are rolling up their ______________ to attract them. Incheon was ______________
(sleeve) (first)
this year to make headlines here for attracting more than 6,000 ______________
(employee)
of a Chinese company called Aurance in March.

FOLLOW-UP ACTIVITY

Complete the following conversations thinking about the appropriate articles such as a, an, some, or the.

1. A : What did you do last Saturday and Sunday?

   B : I saw a movie Saturday and ______________________ Sunday.

   (가족과 피크닉을 갔다.)

   A : Did you have fun?

   B : The picnic was fun, but ______________________.

   (영화는 지루했다.)

2. A : ______________________ was fresh.

   (우리가 그 가게에서 산 과일)

   B : That's the best place to buy fruit.

3. A : I need some gas but ______________________.

   (휘발류가 요즘 비싸다.)

   B : The gas at this gas station is more expensive than the gas at that station.

4. A : I bought a radio. ______________________ when I do house chores.

   (나는 음악 듣기를 좋아한다.)

   B : Would you please turn the radio down? ______________________.

   (음악이 너무 크다.)

   A : No problem.

LIFE IS INTERESTING

Scariest Places on Earth

Roopkund Lake

In 1942 a forest ranger in the Himalayan Mountains of India found a lake that was surrounded by human skeletons. In the summer the ice melted and hundreds more skeletons were found. In 2004 an expedition discovered that all of the people died due to head injuries caused by large round objects. Scientists concluded that they all died from a hail storm. Thousands of baseball sized pieces of frozen rain fell on the people who had nowhere to hide. They can still be seen today.

Karni Mata Temple

This famous Hindu temple in India is crawling with an estimated 20,000 black rats. Thousands of people visit the temple every year to be blessed by the "holy rats." These rats are known as "little children" and are fed milk, grains, coconut shells and sweets. Because food that the rats have touched is said to be good luck, some people eat the leftover snacks.

Island of Haunted Dolls

Mexico's Isla de las Munecas is dedicated to a girl who drowned in the water outside of Mexico City. After her death, dolls began to wash up on the shore of a small island near the place where she died. The island's caretaker, Don Julian, started hanging the dolls from the island's trees in her memory. Locals say the dolls are possessed with the spirit of the dead girl. 50 years after the first dolls were hung on the island, Don Julian was found dead in the same spot where the girl had died. He had drowned.

Q1. If you had to choose one, which of the above places would you visit? Why?

____

Q2. Where is the scariest place in your country? Why?

____

UNIT 02

Try Something New for 30 Days

What Do You Think?

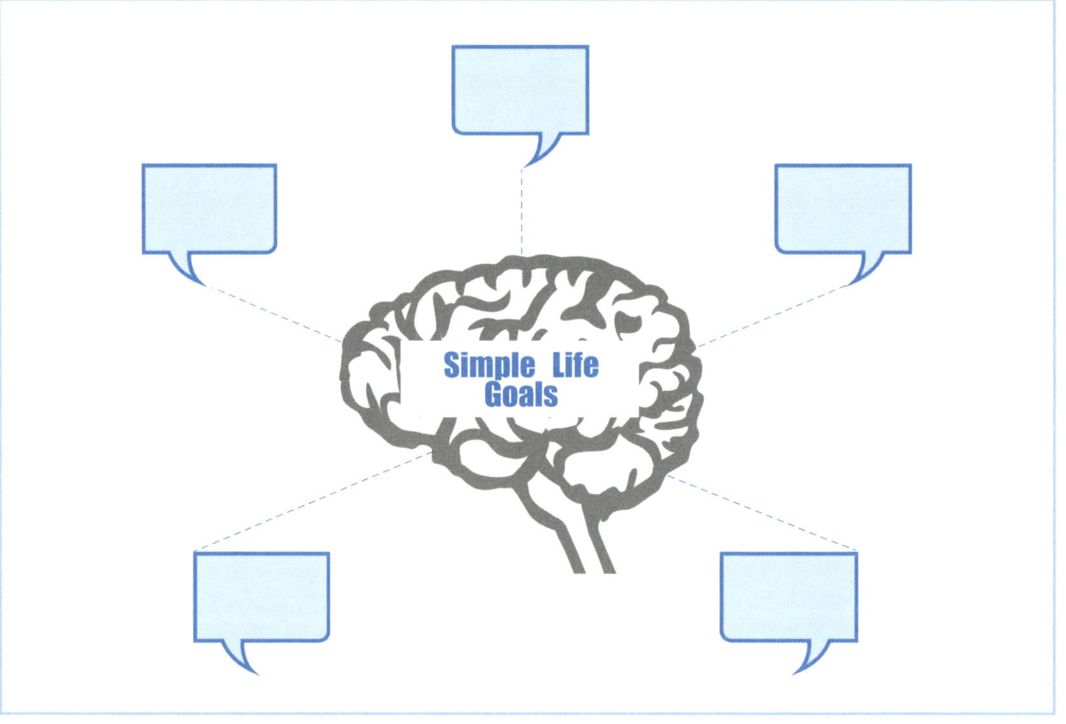

What If?

1. What if you could do any hobby in the world? What would you want to do?

____

____

____

2. What if you wanted to stop a bad habit? How would you do it?

____

____

____

VOCABULARY PREVIEW

1. Read and match the words or phrases with the right meaning.

a. challenge •	• a. reach or come to a certain state
b. self-confidence •	• b. come to understand
c. end up •	• c. a difficult job or task
d. adventurous •	• d. promise given by one person
e. from scratch •	• e. having confidence in oneself
f. figure out •	• f. full of danger and excitement
g. guarantee •	• g. at the beginning

2. Complete the sentences using the words or phrases above.

a. Your report is terrible, start over and write it _______________.

b. Don't worry so much. You'll be O.K. You must have more _______________.

c. I _______________ that he is the most talented person you've ever met.

d. Reducing the gap between poor and rich is one of the main _______________ facing the government.

e. I can't _____________________________ how the machine works.

f. If you drive so fast, you'll _______________ in the hospital.

g. His _______________ life in the jungle is amazing to read about.

Try Something New for 30 Days

Adapted from: Matt Cutts

Sometimes it is easy to get stuck in a rut; to do the same things day after day with no changes or chances for excitement. So, I decided to make a goal for myself of trying something new for 30 days. The idea is actually pretty simple.

First, think about something you've always wanted to add to your life. For example, exercise, reading more, finding new music or foods, etc. Then try that thing for the next 30 days. It turns out that, according to research, 30 days is just about the right amount of time to create a new habit, like watching the news, or to stop a bad habit, like biting your fingernails.

There are a few things I learned while doing these 30-day challenges. The first was that, instead of the months passing by very quickly, and then being forgotten, the time I spent doing these things was much more memorable. Once I challenged myself to take a picture every day for a month. One benefit is that I remember exactly where I was and what I was doing at that time. Completing these challenges has other side effects as well. For example, I noticed that as I did more challenges, and harder challenges, my self-confidence grew.

I began to change as well. In the beginning it seemed like I was living at my desk in the Google main office. I changed into the kind of guy who rides a bicycle to work; for fun! Last year I ended up hiking Mt.

Kilimanjaro, the highest mountain in Africa. I would never have been that adventurous before I started my 30-day challenges.

I've learned that, if you really want something badly enough, you can do anything for 30 days. Have you ever wanted to write a novel? Every November, thousands of people try to write their own 50,000-word novel in 30 days. I figured out that all you need to do is write 1,667 words per day, for a month. So I did. The secret is not to go to sleep until you've written your words for the day. Now is my book a great novel? No. It's awful. However, for the rest of my life, if I want to, I can say "I'm a novelist."

When we make small, simple changes, they are more likely to continue. There's nothing wrong with big, crazy challenges. In fact, they can be very fun, but we are more likely to stop. So, ask yourself, "What am I waiting for?" Certainly, the next 30 days are going to pass by whether you like it or not. So, why not find something you have always wanted to try, and do it! At least for the next 30 days.

READING COMPREHENSION

[A] *Answer the following questions related to the article.*

1. Doing the same things every day, without changes, is called "being ________"
   a. stuck in a rut
   b. stick in the mud
   c. standing around

2. What happened after the speaker did more, and harder, challenges?
   a. He became bored
   b. His confidence grew
   c. He rode a bicycle to work

3. What is the secret to writing 1,667 words per day?
   a. Focus all of your energy.
   b. Get help from your friends.
   c. Don't sleep until you've finished.

4. How long does it take to make a habit?
   a. 13 days
   b. 22 days
   c. 30 days

5. When we make small, simple ________, they are more likely to continue.
   a. challenges
   b. changes
   c. chances

[B] *Answer the questions below with a complete sentence.*

1. What would you like to try doing for 30 days?

____

2. What simple changes could you make to improve your life?

____

[C] *Read the following statements about the article. Answer true or false.*

1. Trying something new for 30 days is difficult. T / F
2. You can make a new habit in 20 days. T / F
3. Taking photos can make our days more memorable. T / F
4. In December thousands of people try to write a novel. T / F
5. Big changes are more likely to continue. T / F

[D] *Fill in the following summary with words from the word bank.*

If you're stuck in a ❶ ____________ you should try to do something new for 30 days. ❷ ____________ days is not too long. In fact, it is just long enough to create a new ❸ ____________ or to stop a bad habit like biting your fingernails. Doing new things can also help your time become more ❹ ____________ and improve your self confidence. In fact, if you really want to do something ❺ ____________ enough, you can do practically ❻ ____________ for 30 days. You could even become a ❼ ____________. The next thirty days are going to pass by no matter what, so why not find something you have always wanted to do and ❽ ____________.

Word Bank

thirty	novelist	habit	badly
do it	anything	rut	memorable

GRAMMAR BUILDER (Pronouns)

Complete the following paragraphs with the words from the list. Each word can be used more than once.

he, him, himself, one, another, the other, the others, they, them, I, me, it, they, myself, something, anything, nothing, anyone

Practice 1

Albert Schweitzer is ______________ of the most famous names in the history of medicine. He decided to become a doctor when he was thirty years old. By this time, he had established ______________ in two other careers, music and theology. In fact, he had already published two books-______________ on the life of Jesus and ______________ on the works of Bach. Even though he became famous in these fields, he gave ______________ up in order to become a doctor and help the sick of Africa.

Practice 2

My life is a full and happy ______________, and I'm grateful for all I've been given. However, I could never call my life perfect when I see so many poor, hungry, and homeless people around ______________. They put up with more difficulties in their lives than I will ever know, and none of ______________ is their fault. How can my conscience not bother me? Isn't it my moral duty to help them? I feel that I'm obligated to do ______________ and blame ______________ every day for doing ______________. But what one thing can I do to relieve their pain? Can ______________ tell me? Can you?

FOLLOW-UP ACTIVITY

Complete the following conversations using the appropriate pronouns.

1. A : I have a book somewhere. Is this my book?

B : No, it belongs to Tom. ________________________________.

(나는 너의 것은 저기 있다고 생각한다.)

2. A : I need a red pen. ________________________________?

(내가 빌릴 수 있는 것을 가지고 있나요?)

B : No. ________________________________.

(Mary가 가지고 있는지 물어봐.)

3. A : Where is my Korean-English dictionary? I need it.

B : I don't know. ________________________________?

(너 그것을 누군가에게 빌려주지 않았니?)

4. A : Tom has made a lot of progress in English. Last semester he couldn't order a meal in a restaurant.

B : Yeah. ________________________________.

(그의 친구들이 그가 하는 모든 것을 도와주었다.)

Now he can speak English in a lot of situations.

5. A : I heard there was a fire in your apartment yesterday. ______________?

(누군가 다쳤니?)

B : No. The firefighters ________________________________.

(소방관들이 모두를 빌딩 밖으로 내보냈다.)

6. A : Where did you get those new running shoes? They look comfortable.

B : ________________________________.

(Sam's Sport Shop에서 찾았어.)

LIFE IS INTERESTING

Benefits of Laughter

Strengthens Relationships

Laughter can help in just about every social situation. It makes people feel more comfortable and can help people bond. In your closest relationships - those with your partner, parents or children - laughter is very important, but it is also important with people you do not know well. When you laugh, others will want to be with you and work with you, which is often a good thing.

Relieves stress and helps with relaxation

It is hard to feel angry, upset, anxious or afraid while laughing. That is because it is a natural way to deal with stress. It can often make you see things differently and makes stressful situations and experiences easier to deal with. It also relieves physical tension.

Keeps you healthy

Scientists have been linking laughter to general health for decades. For example, laughing for a few minutes per day has a similar effect on the body as a light workout. Laughter is also thought to give a helping hand to your immune system. Of course you should not replace doctor visits with laughing, but laughing can't do any harm and might even be doing good things for you.

Q1. What is something that always makes you laugh?

____

Q2. Of all the people you know, who has the best laugh? How does it make you feel?

____

UNIT 03

The Best Gift I Ever Survived

What Do You Think?

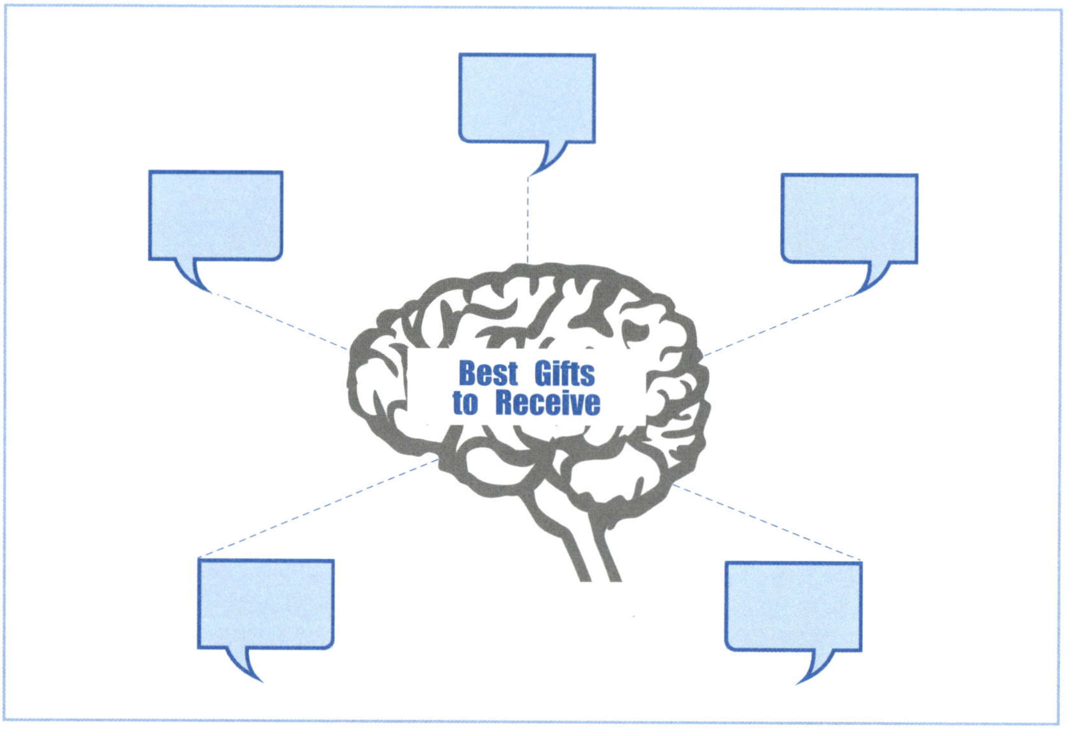

What If?

1. What if you could change your life? What would you change?

____

____

____

2. What if you only had 6 months to live? What would you do with your time?

____

____

____

VOCABULARY PREVIEW

1. **Read and match the words or phrases with the right meaning.**

a. incredible •	• a. very useful
b. appreciate •	• b. abnormal mass of new tissue
c. tumor •	• c. impossible to believe
d. inspire •	• d. frightening
e. motivate •	• e. fill somebody with influence
f. valuable •	• f. value highly
g. scary •	• g. cause somebody to work

2. **Complete the sentences using the words or phrases above.**

a. I gained some ______________ experience from volunteer work.

b. My father needs an operation to remove a ______________ in his left lung.

c. He earned an ______________ amount of money after launching a startup.

d. Watching young drivers go so fast is a little ______________.

e. His work can ______________ the rest of his coworkers to do better.

f. I really ______________ your help.

g. The teacher always ______________ his students to work harder.

The Best Gift I Ever Survived

Adapted from: Stacey Kramer

Gifts can come in many different shapes and sizes. Gifts can also come from anywhere, at any time, and some of the best ones are unexpected. The best gifts are not always items, but can also be experiences or moments in time. Furthermore, some gifts don't appear to be gifts at all until much later.

Six months ago I received a life changing gift, the size of a golf ball, inside of a very special gift bag. This gift did incredible things for me, like bringing my family closer together, and making me feel loved and appreciated like never before. My life changing gift also helped me reconnect with old friends and rethink what was important in my life.

The gift I received is not something that you can buy in a store. In the United States it costs around $55,000, which is a good price. This gift increased my vocabulary, helped me become more healthy and caused people to tell me, "You look great. Did you get plastic surgery?" My gift was not something I could buy in a store, but instead was something that happened to me. I got a brain tumor.

In 2015, I received a special red bag with a "Biohazard" warning on the outside. Prior to that, I got to see an X-ray picture of it, and received a large scar on my neck. These days I am more than okay. Having this tumor made me feel challenged, inspired, and motivated. Learning about the tumor helped give my life new meaning and taught me to be full of peace, and happiness.

I would never wish for anyone to receive this type of gift, although I would never change my experience, even if I could. Most people would agree that having a brain tumor does not sound like a gift. However, while it was a very scary experience, the benefits I received because of it are more valuable than any gift I have gotten in my life.

Bad things happen to people every day. Something bad has probably happened to you, or sadly, will happen to you in the future. Having a bad thing happen to you doesn't mean that your experience needs to be negative. Sometimes bad things can turn out to be the best things in our lives.

READING COMPREHENSION

[A] *Answer the following questions related to the article.*

1. What is the cost of Stacey Kramer's "gift?"

a. Five thousand five hundred dollars

b. Fifty-five hundred dollars

c. Fifty-five thousand dollars

2. What kind of picture did she receive?

a. Selfie

b. X-ray

c. Painting

3. Where can you buy a "gift" like this one?

a. On the Internet

b. You cannot buy one

c. In a department store

4. This gift is going to do __________ things for you.

a. important

b. incredible

c. interesting

5. The speaker received her gift __________ months ago.

a. Three

b. Four

c. Five

d. Six

[B] *Answer the questions below with a complete sentence.*

1. What event has changed your life the most?

____

2. What is the best gift you ever received?

____

[C] *Read the following statements about the article. Answer true or false.*

1. The "gift" will make your family less close. T / F
2. The best gifts are always items. T / F
3. The author seems like a very negative person. T / F
4. The author's "gift" came in a green bag. T / F
5. The author received a large scar on her arm. T / F

[D] *Fill in the following summary with words from the word bank.*

If you are faced with something ❶ ____________ or unwanted in your life it is not always a bad thing. Sometimes these bad things can be a ❷ ____________ They can help bring your family and friends ❸ ____________ to you. Bad things can also help you improve your feelings about life and ❹ ____________ new people. Sometimes bad things can even help you change your ❺ ____________ and learn to ❻ ____________ the world around you. Bad things don't always have to be ❼ ____________, in fact, sometimes bad things can lead to ❽ ____________ changes in your life.

Word Bank

closer	lifestyle	gift	meet
positive	appreciate	unexpected	negative

GRAMMAR BUILDER (Verbs)

Complete the following paragraphs using the words in parentheses. Change verb forms if needed. For example, simple present, simple past, or present perfect.

Practice 1

She ______________ (fall) down stairs on Feb. 15, breaking a rib that then pierced one of her lungs. She ______________ (hospitalize) after the fall, but ______________ (be) still in serious condition. At the age of 17, she ______________ (send) to a military brothel in China. After Korea's liberation from Japanese occupation in 1945, she ______________ (stay) in China and ______________ (marry) a Chinese man.

Practice 2

Many modern marriages are finding interesting solutions to difficult problems. Take Mr. Kim and Ms. Lee, for example. They ______________ (marry) in March 2012. They ______________ (live) in Seoul for 2 years together before Mr. Kim moved to Pusan. In 2014 Mr. Kim ______________ (get) a great job offer from a company in Pusan and ______________ (go) there alone. As Ms. Lee's company is in Seoul, they ______________ (live) apart ever since. They ______________ (travel) back and forth between Seoul and Pusan now. Sociologists call this kind of marriage a "commuter marriage". "It ______________ (not easy)" says Ms. Lee. "Last month I ______________ (see) Mr. Kim four times, but this month I ______________ (only see) him once."

FOLLOW-UP ACTIVITY

Look at Tom's schedule and complete the sentences below.
Use a proper verb tense such as simple present, simple past, present progressive.

Tom's Schedule

7:00 a.m – 8:00 a.m get to work 8:00 a.m – 10:00 a.m check e-mails 10:00 a.m – 12:00 p.m meet and consult with my clients	12:00 p.m – 1:00 p.m have lunch 1:00 p.m – 4:00 p.m write reports and send them to the manager 4:00 p.m – 5:00 p.m return phone calls 6:00 p.m – 7:00 p.m arrive home

1. Tom usually ________________________________.
(Tom은 7시에서 8시 사이에 직장에 도착한다.)

2. It's 8:30 a.m At the moment, he ________________________.
(그는 지금 이메일을 확인하고 있다.)

3. It's 12:00 p.m He ________________________ since 10:00 a.m.
(그는 10시 이후로 고객을 만나고 상담을 하고 있다.)

4. He ________________________ at a restaurant. It's 1:30 p.m.
(그의 동료들과 식당에서 식사를 했다.)

5. He ________________________________ every day.
(그는 매일 3시간을 보고서를 쓰고 팀장에게 보내는데 사용한다.)

6. What does he ________________________________?
(4시와 5시 사이에 그는 무엇을 하나?)

7. When he met and consulted with his clients, ________________.
(그는 이미 이메일을 확인했다.)

LIFE IS INTERESTING

Crazy Laws

For over 200 years it was illegal for women in France to wear pants

In 1799, a Parisian law made it illegal for women to wear pants in public without special approval from the police. It was once changed in 1892 to let women wear pants while riding horses and again in 1909 to permit ladies to wear pants while on bicycles. Finally in 2013, the French government removed this 214-year-old law.

Being overweight is illegal in Japan

In the country that brought the world the art of Sumo wrestling there is something known as a "metabo law." It says all men and women over the age of 40 must not have a waist measuring over 81cm and 91cm respectively. For citizens there is no penalty or punishment. The law is aimed at putting pressure on local governments and companies.

Chewing gum is illegal in Singapore

Chewing gum can send you to prison in Singapore. Chewing gum has been completely illegal in Singapore since 1992. There is also a ban on importing chewing gum into the country. Under the rule only nicotine gum is allowed, but even then, the only way to get gum is to have a doctor's prescription. No gum is allowed to be bought or sold inside Singapore and there is a $500 fine for spitting out gum on the streets.

Q1. What is one law in your country that you do not like? Why?

____

Q2. If you could make one new law for your country, what would it be?

____

UNIT 04

Success is a Continuous Journey

What Do You Think?

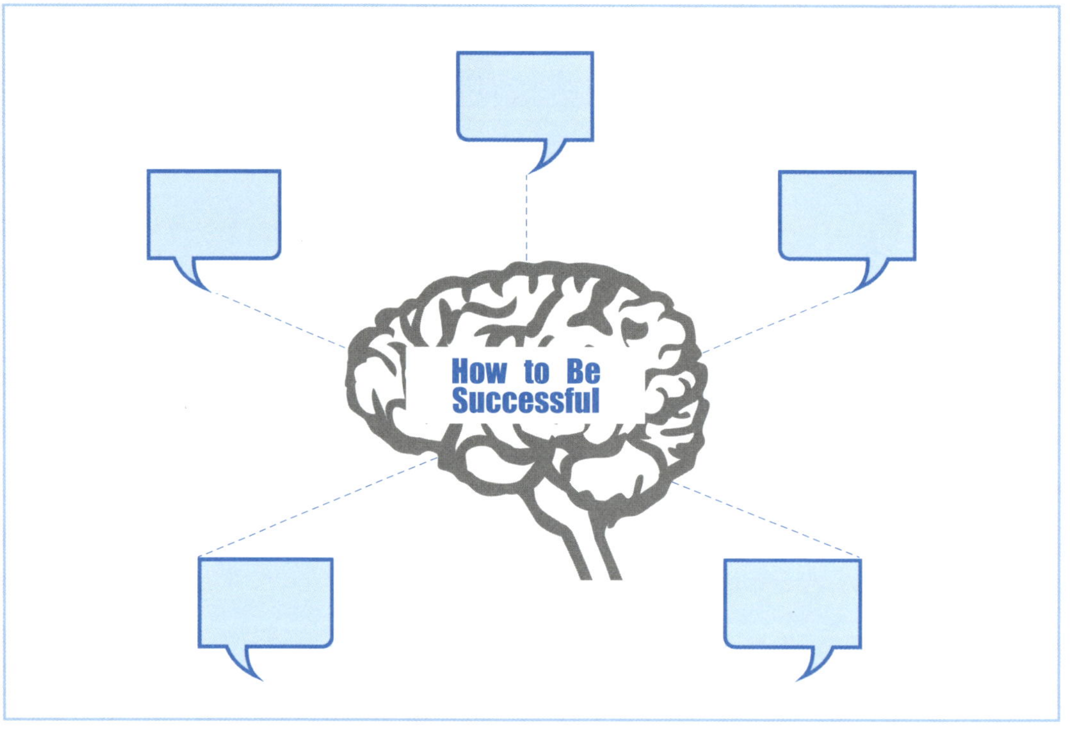

What If?

1. What if you could be the best at anything? What would you choose?

____

____

____

2. What if you became successful and then failed? What would you do?

____

____

____

VOCABULARY PREVIEW

1. Read and match the words or phrases with the right meaning.

a. make it •	• a. on the surface
b. be good at •	• b. prevent from concentrating on something
c. come up with •	• c. be able to perform satisfactorily
d. work at •	• d. engage in physical or mental activity
e. pour in •	• e. be successful in one's career
f. distract •	• f. come or go in a continuous stream
g. outwardly •	• g. find or produce

2. Complete the sentences using the words or phrases above.

a. It is too bad that he will never really ______________ as an actor.
b. Ms. Lee appeared ______________ calm even though she was badly surprised.
c. I find it difficult to study at home since my children ______________ me.
d. If you'd like to ______________ a foreign language, patience and diligence are necessary.
e. My sister has been ______________ her project all day.
f. Every morning commuters ______________ to the subway station.
g. He should ______________ a new idea for increasing sales in China.

Success is a Continuous Journey

Adapted from: Richard St. John

Why do so many people become successful and then fail? One of the big reasons is that most people think success is a one-way street. We do everything that leads up to success, but when we get there we sit in our comfort zone, and actually stop doing everything that made us successful. Once that occurs, it doesn't take long for things to begin to fail. I know that this situation happens because it happened to me.

I worked very hard in order to become a success, but then I stopped because I thought, "I made it. I can sit back and relax." When I was trying to become successful, I was good at coming up with ideas. Then I stopped because I began to feel that I shouldn't have to work at ideas, they should just come to me like magic. However, the only thing that came to me was a creative block; I couldn't think of new ideas.

Eventually, a black cloud formed over my head. On the outside I appeared to be very successful, but on the inside I was very depressed. As a man I thought I knew how to fix my unhappiness, so I bought a fast car, but it didn't help. I was able to go faster but I was still depressed. Next, I went to my doctor. I said, "I can buy anything I want, but I'm not happy. It's true what they say, money can't buy happiness." My doctor then put me on anti-depressants.

Not too long after this situation my clients began to feel that I was no longer serving them, and that I was only serving myself. They took their money and their projects to other people who would serve them better. Soon after this event my business began to fail and we had to fire our employees. Truthfully, that was a good thing. I went back to doing the projects I loved and I had fun again. I worked harder and did all the things that made me a success. I became successful once again, but it took me seven years.

In the end, my business grew bigger than ever, the black cloud over my head disappeared, and I didn't need drugs anymore. I learned that success is a continuous journey. To avoid "success-to-failure-syndrome," we just need to keep going forward. Life is not only about how we achieve success, but also how we sustain it.

READING COMPREHENSION

[A] *Answer the following questions related to the article.*

1. What is the main idea of this speech?
   a. Being successful is a continuous journey.
   b. Anyone can become successful easily.
   c. When you're unhappy, buying things can help.

2. If you have a "black cloud" over your head you are __________.
   a. tired
   b. depressed
   c. busy

3. How long did it take for the author to become successful again?
   a. five years
   b. nine Years
   c. seven years

4. According to the reading most people think "success is a __________ street."
   a. dead-end
   b. one-way
   c. two-lane

5. When he was depressed, the author had a __________ cloud over his head.
   a. blue
   b. black
   c. rain

[B] *Answer the questions below with a complete sentence.*

1. What is your definition of success?

   ____

2. Have you ever felt depressed? How did you start to feel better?

   ____

[C] *Read the following statements about the article. Answer true or false.*

1. Success is a one-way street. T / F
2. Ideas should come to people easily; like magic. T / F
3. Firing employees was a good thing for the author. T / F
4. Being successful is not a continuous journey. T / F
5. Life is about achieving and sustaining success. T / F

[D] *Fill in the following summary with words from the word bank.*

Becoming ❶ ______________ is not an easy thing to do. Continuing to be successful is even more difficult. Many people ❷ ______________ a success due to hard work, but once they become successful they begin to change their ❸ ______________. This change can lead these people to fail. Once you start to lose your success it is very easy to become ❹ ______________ and unhappy which has even more negative ❺ ______________ on your life. Working hard to ❻ ______________ success is important, but ❼ ______________ to work hard and move ❽ ______________ is also very important.

Word Bank

depressed	achieve	behavior	continuing
forward	become	successful	effects

GRAMMAR BUILDER (Subject-Verb Agreement)

Complete the following paragraphs using the words in parentheses. Change verb forms if needed.

Practice 1

Slightly more than 24 percent of households in Seoul ______________ (be) made up of just one person. The latest figures regarding household sizes in Seoul during 2010 ______________ (be) released in the March edition of "Seoul Economics", a monthly news letter which ______________ (be) published by the Seoul Metropolitan Government. The figure ______________ (be) only 4.5 percent in 1980. The chief of the Global Future Research Center of the Seoul Institute who conducted the survey, said the rise ______________ (be) mainly attributable to the increase in women's economic activities and the change of their views on marriage, which led to the growth of women choosing to remain single or marry at a later age.

Practice 2

Office worker Lee, 28, ______________ (wish) to keep working after marriage. Such an idea has become widespread among young women over the past decade, as female participation in the workforce ______________ (have grown) significantly. "In many cases young men ______________ (prefer) to have their spouses work, so that both can contribute to household finances," male office worker Kim, 29, said. Figures ______________ (back) this trend–according to data from Statistics Korea, the number of women who ______________ (marry) without jobs or being students dropped from 169,581 in 2005 to 102,915 in 2015.

FOLLOW-UP ACTIVITY

Complete the following sentences thinking about subject-verb agreement.

1. One of my friends ____.

(매일 학교까지 자전거를 탄다.)

2. ______________________________________ to be answered this morning.

(중요한 질문들이 있다.)

3. Economics ____.

(나에게는 어려운 과목이다.)

4. The book about the American fifty states ____________________.

(재미있어서 나는 그것을 다른 사람에게 추천하고 싶다.)

5. Local news ____.

(매일 밤 11시에 TV에서 방송한다.)

6. Everyone ____.

(오늘 밤 영화를 보러 갈 것이다.)

7. Each member of my family ______________________________.

(멕시코 음식을 좋아한다.)

8. ____ is twelve.

(이 수업의 학생의 수는)

9. Most of the food at the cafeteria ____________________________.

(맛있다.)

10. Five thousand miles ______________________________________.

(너무 멀어서 차로 여행할 수 없다.)

LIFE IS INTERESTING

Legendary Lost Cities

The City of Troy

The city of Troy is thought to be nothing more than a myth. Troy was the capital of the Trojan empire. It was the site of a legendary war between the Greek and Trojan armies which started when the famous Greek beauty Helen was captured. It might be a myth, but in the 19th century ruins were found that many believe is the lost city of Troy.

El Dorado: The Lost City of Gold

For a city that almost surely never existed, El Dorado has consumed a lot of real blood and treasure. This is because El Dorado is said to be filled with treasure. Many 16th century explorers thought this "City of Gold" was somewhere in Central America. Famous adventurers such as Gonzalo Pizarro and Sir Walter Raleigh undertook massive expeditions in search of the city, only to come away with nothing.

Atlantis

Plato described Atlantis as a mighty island city filled with strong, brave, intelligent citizens. The island of Atlantis was said to have sunk into the sea in less than a day. Many believe Plato was speaking figuratively, and the island never really existed. This has not stopped generations of explorers from searching for the lost city. People claim to have found Atlantis in places ranging from the Mediterranean Sea to the coast of Florida.

Q1. **If you found a city made of gold, what is the first thing you would buy? Why?**

____

Q2. **Do you believe that Atlantis was a real place or is it just a story? Why?**

____

UNIT 05

How to Start a Movement

What Do You Think?

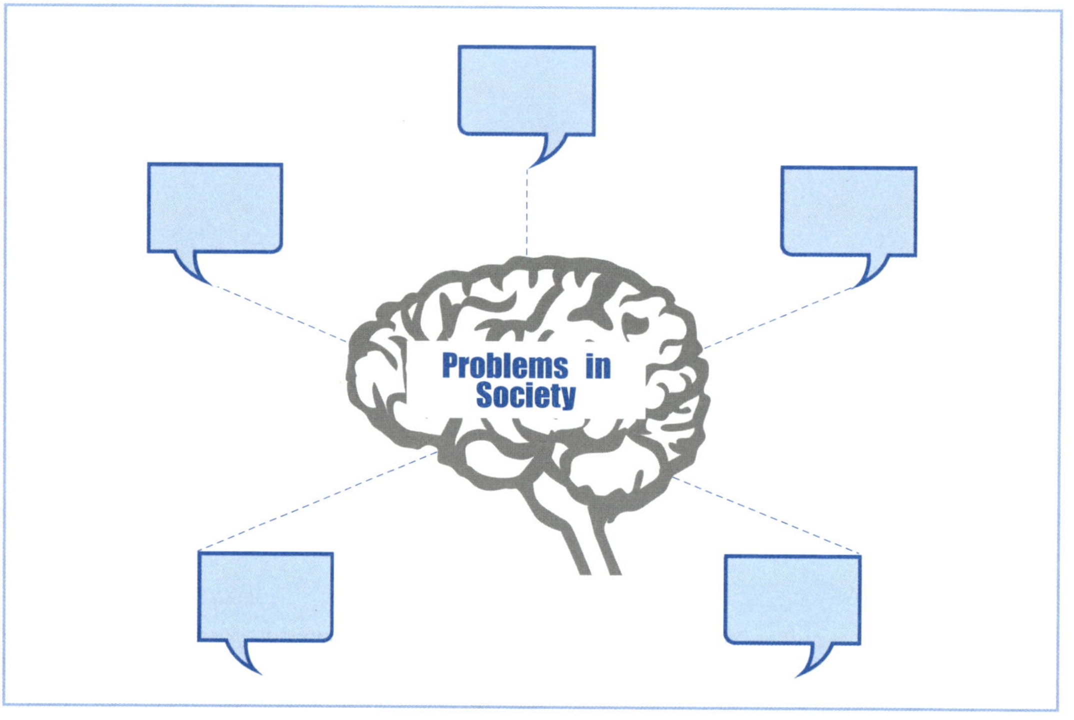

What If?

1. What if you had the power to change anything in your country? What would you change?

____

____

____

2. What if someone had a good idea, but your friends think this person is crazy? Who would you follow?

____

____

____

VOCABULARY PREVIEW

1. **Read and match the words with the right meaning.**

a. courage •	• a. make too low an estimate
b. relatively •	• b. cause people to laugh at
c. embrace •	• c. ability to control fear
d. underestimate •	• d. accept or take willingly
e. transform ~ into •	• e. completely change
f. stand out •	• f. be easily seen
g. make fun of •	• g. to a particular degree, especially when compared to something similar

2. **Complete the sentences using the words or phrases above.**

a. It is bad to ______________ people who are disabled.

b. Don't ______________ others. They may be better than you.

c. I don't have the ______________ to say 'no' when someone asks me to do something I don't like to do.

d. It is time to ______________ his idea and change.

e. I work up ______________ early this morning.

f. The yellow lettering on the sign ______________ well against a dark background.

g. We need to ______________ the area from a desert ______________ a swamp.

How to Start a Movement

Adapted from: Derek Sivers

In our modern society, making changes takes a great amount of effort and a long time. There are people who talk about creating a movement in order to create change in our world. Movements require leadership, surely, but having a strong leader is not enough. Creating a movement requires a few key elements.

First, a leader needs the courage to stand out and be teased and ridiculed. People may even think that a leader is strange simply because they are different. However, what a leader is doing can be relatively easy to follow. The next important role after a leader is the first follower; this person is going to show everyone else how to follow.

In a successful movement the leader will embrace the follower as an equal. When this happens the movement is no longer just about the leader; it's about them, plural. Next, the follower will talk to his or her friends. In this way, the first follower is actually an underestimated form of leadership in itself. The first follower is what transforms a lone person with new ideas into a leader.

Once the first follower has connected to their friends a second follower can join the movement. We say that three is a crowd, and in our modern media centered world, a crowd is news. A movement must be public. It's important to show not just the leader, but also the followers, because we have found that new followers copy other followers, not the leader.

Soon there will be others who join the movement because, as more people join in, becoming part of the group is less risky for new people. People that were unsure before, now have no reason not to join. New people won't stand out, and they won't be teased. Moreover, they will be part of the movement's center if they hurry. Eventually we will see that people will join because they would be made fun of for not joining. Once we have reached this tipping point, we have created a powerful movement that can change society.

If you really care about starting a movement, have the courage to follow and show others how to follow. And when you find a lone person doing something great, even if it appears to be strange, have the courage to be the first one to stand up and join in.

READING COMPREHENSION

[A] *Answer the following questions related to the article.*

1. Movements require __________.
   a. money
   b. volunteers
   c. leaders

2. "Three is a crowd" and a crowd is __________?
   a. noisy
   b. news
   c. necessary

3. For a movement to be successful, what is most important?
   a. followers
   b. friends
   c. fellows

4. How much time is usually required to change society?
   a. Case by case
   b. Not much time
   c. A long time

5. What makes it less risky for people to join a movement?
   a. A strong leader with an original idea
   b. More people becoming part of the group
   c. A first follower that knows how to follow

[B] *Answer the questions below with a complete sentence.*

1. Are you comfortable being a leader? Why or why not?

____

2. Who have you followed in your life? Why?

____

[C] *Read the following statements about the article. Answer true or false.*

1.	In society we can make changes quickly.	T / F
2.	Leaders need courage.	T / F
3.	In a movement, leaders should embrace followers.	T / F
4.	Powerful movements can change society.	T / F
5.	Following takes courage also.	T / F

[D] *Fill in the following summary with words from the word bank.*

Sometimes society needs to change. One way to change things is by creating a ❶ ____________. Movements require a few ❷ ____________ elements. Firstly, there must be a leader with the ❸ ____________ to be different. Next, we need someone who is not afraid to follow the leader. This first follower has a very important role, because they show other people how to follow the ❹ ____________. These two people will find more and more people. ❺ ____________, you will be strange if you do not become part of this new movement. When that happens, the movement is truly ❻ ____________ and society can ❼ ____________. The first step is to be a leader, or have the courage to be a ❽ ____________.

Word Bank

key	change	eventually	follower
leader	courage	powerful	movement

GRAMMAR BUILDER (Adjectives/ Adverbs)

Complete the following paragraphs using the words in parentheses. Change word forms if needed.

Practice 1

Sixty-five children were killed in car accidents last year, up 25 percent from a year earlier. ________________ 80 percent of the ________________ accidents were reported
(near) (dead)
in or ________________ crosswalks in school zones, according to police data. Children's
(near)
lack of attention to approaching vehicles can be considered one reason. Another is
________________ or ________________ driving in school zones.
(speed) (care)

Practice 2

The Ministry of Health and Welfare recommended eating a variety of ________________
(nutrition)
food including rice, whole grains, fruits, milk, dairy products, meat, fish, eggs and beans to ensure a ________________ and ________________ diet. At the same time,
(balance) (health)
it called on people to avoid overeating and to do more ________________ activities
(physical)
and exercise. In addition, the guidelines asked people to use more ________________ --
(local)
________________ ________________ products.
(grow) (agriculture)

FOLLOW-UP ACTIVITY

Complete the following letter. Each sentence should have one or more adjectives or adverbs.

Dear Mom and Dad,

______________________. Since I have never left my small hometown,
(N.Y 생활은 매우 재미있습니다.)

______________________________ like N.Y before coming here.
(나는 뉴욕과 같은 큰 도시에 사는 것이 두려웠습니다)

I also wasn't sure ______________________________, but I can. I love it.
(나는 당신들 없이 살 수 있을지)

You'd be surprised to see me. I walk happily down the busy street, and the noise doesn't bother me at all. There is always something to do.

Yesterday, on my way home, ______________________________.
(나는 멋진 거리 악사를 보았습니다.)

______________________________.
(그는 너무 아름답게 바이올린을 연주했습니다.)

I couldn't believe he was on the street and not in a big concert hall.

______________________________.
(한국에서 온 새로운 룸메이트는 친절하고 예쁩니다.)

She seemed to be shy at first and ______________________________.
(거의 말하지 않았습니다.)

Now we can't stop talking and now ______________________________.
(우리는 지금 매우 좋은 친구입니다.)

______________________________.
(부모님 두 분 다 잘 지내시길 바랍니다.)

Please give my love to everyone and write back soon!

Wendy

LIFE IS INTERESTING

Know When to Break up with Your Job

It keeps you alone

Spending time at work is normal, but a job that gently convinces you to stay all the time is a warning sign. Do you find yourself there more than half of your day? Does your job limit your contact with friends and family? If so, it may be time to look for something else. No one died wishing they had spent more time at work.

It uses money to control your behavior

Abusive jobs use money for control. Beware of jobs where over 50% of your income is based on performance, especially if your performance is judged by your boss.

It constantly puts you down

Feedback is a good thing. Constantly being told to improve is not. You are not perfect, but neither is your job. When things go wrong, it is not only your fault. A job is often more than just one person so all people should be responsible for their part.

It controls your appearance

Having a uniform or clothing policy is pretty standard. It is part of a business's image. However, truly controlling jobs will attempt to have an opinion on every aspect of your look. In extreme cases, jobs may even tell you to lose weight. If you need to severely adjust your normal appearance for a job, then maybe that job is not for you.

Q1. Have you, or someone you know, quit their job? Why?

____

Q2. When you have a job, how can the company keep you happy? What do you need?

____

UNIT 06

Got a Meeting? Take a Walk.

What Do You Think?

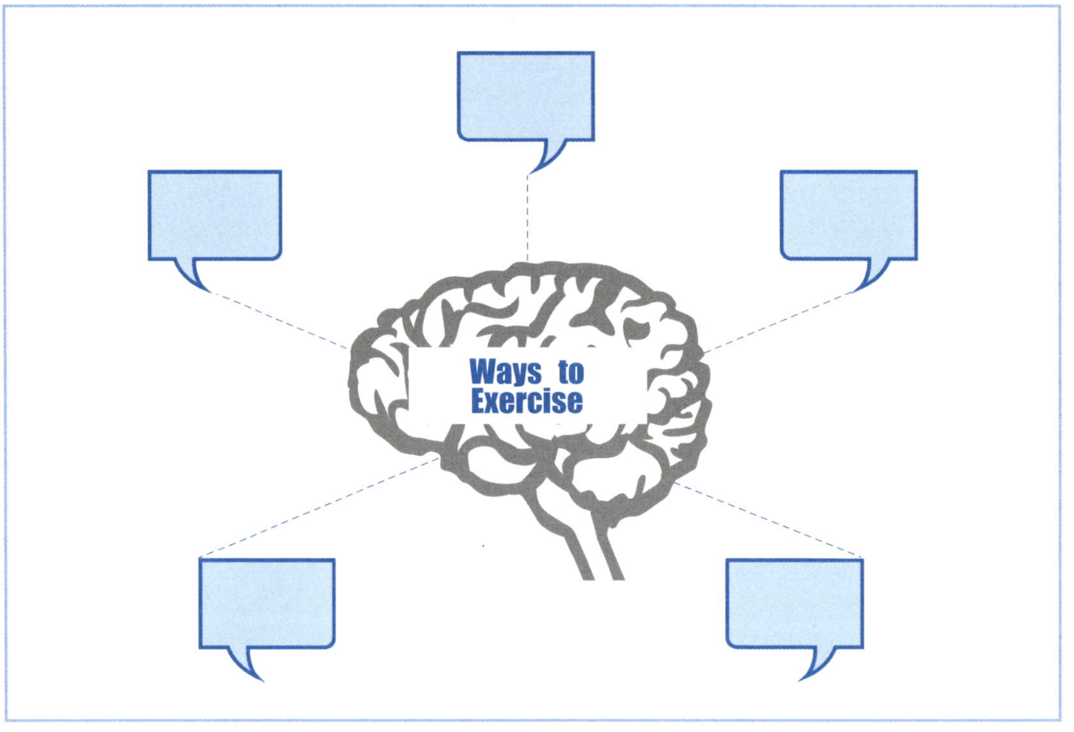

What If?

1. What if you needed to lose 30kg in one year? What would you do?

____

____

____

2. What if you couldn't sit down anymore? How would that affect your life?

____

____

____

VOCABULARY PREVIEW

1. Read and match the words or phrases with the right meaning.

a. generation •	• a. make somebody feel certain
b. consequence •	• b. involving the loss or sacrifice of something
c. convince •	• c. thing that is a result
d. bottom line •	• d. breathe heavily
e. huff and puff •	• e. all people born at about the same time
f. at the cost of •	• f. keep alive
g. sustainable •	• g. essential point

2. Complete the sentences using the words or phrases above.

a. How can you ______________ me that you are innocent?

b. She saved her son from the fire, but ______________ her own life.

c. The decision you made could have serious ______________ for the company.

d. He is ______________ since he ran to catch the bus.

e. There is a ______________ gap between the young and the old.

f. The ______________ is that you're just not good enough.

g. Fresh water is less ______________ now than 40 years ago.

Got a Meeting? Take a Walk.

Adapted from: Nilofer Merchant

For most people, what you're probably doing right now, at this very moment, is killing you. More than cars or the Internet or even the mobile devices we use constantly. What's killing you is sitting on your butt. Nowadays, people are sitting 9.3 hours a day. The average person only sleeps for 7.7 hours. Sitting is so incredibly common we don't even question how much we're doing it. Also, because everyone else is doing it, it doesn't even occur to us that it's not okay. Sitting has become the smoking of our generation.

Sitting down too much has many scary health consequences besides gaining weight. Diseases like breast cancer and colon cancer are directly tied to our lack of physical activity. In fact, sitting too much increases our chances of getting these by up to 10%. The risk for heart diseases increases by six percent and seven percent for type 2 diabetes. You might think that these statistics should convince each of us to get off our tush more, but if you're anything like me, they won't.

While scary statistics should be enough to get us moving, what finally got me going was social interaction. I once had a person invite me to a meeting, but she couldn't find a time in her office. So she said, "I have to walk my dogs tomorrow. Could you come then?" It seemed kind of odd, and I was worried because I needed to do a lot of talking, and I knew I was going to huff and puff during this conversation. However, I enjoyed the experience so much, that I've taken that idea and made it my own. So I've started asking people to go on walking meetings and it has changed my life.

Before I started walking during meetings, I used to think that people could only take care of their health or their busy schedule, but not both. One always came at the cost of the other. Now, after several hundred of these walking meetings, I've learned a few things.

First, there seems to be this amazing thing about being outdoors that leads to out-of-the-box thinking. Whether it's nature, or the exercise itself, it works. Secondly, I learned that we often think our problems work against each other, but it's not actually true. We need the ability to think about those problems in a way that makes them separate. Because, when that happens things become doable and sustainable. The bottom line is, walk and talk. You'll be surprised how fresh air drives fresh thinking, and if you do, you'll bring new ideas into your life.

READING COMPREHENSION

[A] *Answer the following questions related to the article.*

1. What's killing more people than cars and technology?

a. sitting

b. drugs

c. cancer

2. How much time are people sitting every day?

a. Just under nine hours

b. Almost eight hours

c. A little over nine hours

3. Sitting too much has become the ___________ of our generation.

a. drinking

b. laziness

c. smoking

4. What kind of meetings have changed the author's life?

a. short meetings

b. telephone meetings

c. walking meetings

5. What can lead to out-of-the-box thinking?

a. meeting new people

b. being outside

c. trying new things

[B] *Answer the questions below with a complete sentence.*

1. What can you do to sit less during the day?

____

2. How can you balance a healthy life and being busy?

____

[C] *Read the following statements about the article. Answer true or false.*

1. People are sitting too much these days. T / F
2. Some people are sleeping more than sitting. T / F
3. Sitting too much increases the risks of some diseases. T / F
4. People cannot be healthy and busy at the same time. T / F
5. Fresh air does not help people think. T / F

[D] *Fill in the following summary with words from the word bank.*

In today's world people are on their ❶ ______________ too much. In fact, many people sit longer, per day, than they ❷ ______________. This behavior can increase our risks for things like ❸ ______________, heart disease and diabetes. Some people think that you can't take care of your health and be busy at the same time. ❹ ______________, it is possible. One small change is to ❺ ______________ when you are meeting with people. Having walking ❻ ______________ can increase your ability to think ❼ ______________ and come up with new ideas. It is possible to make positive changes in your life when you learn to view your problems ❽ ______________ and not together as one big issue.

Word Bank

walk	butts	however	meetings
separately	cancer	creatively	sleep

GRAMMAR BUILDER (Participles)

Complete the following paragraphs using the words in parentheses. Change verb forms if needed.

Practice 1

A pediatrician and nutritionist at a medical center said ______________ sugar intake from
(minimize)
an early age is crucial in ______________ and ______________ healthy ______________
(establish) (maintain) (eat)
habits. "Once children get used to the sweetness of sugar in food, they are less likely to eat vegetables and fruits or other healthy foods that do not taste so sweet," she said. It is not good that many children and teenagers consume sugar in such large amounts.

Practice 2

The government has issued dietary guidelines in the hope of ______________ people's
(improve)
______________ habits by ______________ them to consume less salty, sweet and
(eat) (get)
fatty foods and keep a ______________ diet. The measure came a day after the government
(balance)
declared a campaign against excessive sugar consumption, pointing out that Koreans' sugar intake has neared an ______________ level. Sugar is cited as a major cause
(alarm)
of obesity and diabetes among Koreans.

FOLLOW-UP ACTIVITY

Complete each sentence with the participial adjective that comes from the underlined verb.

For example : The movie bored me.
→ The movie was boring and I was bored. (영화가 지루해서 나는 지루했다.)

1. The garbage in the hallway disgusted Mary.
→ The garbage ____________________ and Mary ____________________.
(쓰레기가 역겨워서 Mary는 역겨웠다.)

2. The subway ride exhausts Sue.
→ ____________________ because the subway ride ____________________.
(지하철 타는 것이 피곤해서 Sue는 피곤함을 느낀다.)

3. Those appetizers in the restaurant didn't satisfy me.
→ As the appetizers ____________________, ____________________.
(에피타이저는 만족스럽지 못해서 나는 만족하지 못했다.)

4. Tom's travel stories always amaze us.
→ His stories ____________________ so ____________________.
(그의 이야기들은 놀라워서 우리는 놀랐다.)

5. I don't speak English well at all and my mistakes embarrassed me.
→ ____.
(나는 약간의 당황스러운 실수 때문에 당황했다.)

6. His lecture confused his students.
→ Since ____.
(그의 강의는 혼란스러워서 그의 학생들은 혼란스러웠다.)

LIFE IS INTERESTING

Gross Flies

Buffy Flies

What do toads and frogs eat? They eat flies, right? The Buffy fly hates that. Buffy flies lay their eggs in the head of live toads. Buffy flies put their eggs right into the toad's nose. It's definitely disgusting, but we should admire the courage of this fly to get that close to a toad's mouth. Also, this is a very safe place for their babies to grow.

Small-headed Flies

"Small-headed flies," also known as Acroceridae, are very cute little bugs. They don't bite, or sting and they only drink flower nectar. In fact, they slightly resemble the fly version of a bumble bee. Their babies can move quickly and even jump. As soon as they hatch from their eggs, they look for spiders. Once they find a large one, they make a home in its shell for up to 10 years. Poor little spiders.

Congo Floor Maggot

The Congo Floor Maggot is one of the worst for humans. This bug lives in the dirt floors of huts in sub-Saharan Africa. At night they come out of the ground and try to bite human feet. Luckily they are only found in places with dirt floors that can easily be covered by mats.

Note : If you're interested in gross flies, there is one fly that is the worst. It's known as the Sheep Nose Bot Fly. Don't search online for this fly after eating. You've been warned.

Q1. Which of these three flies is the most disgusting to you? What makes it so gross?

____

Q2. What types of bugs are you afraid of? Why do you think that is?

____

UNIT 07

Eight Secrets to Success

What Do You Think?

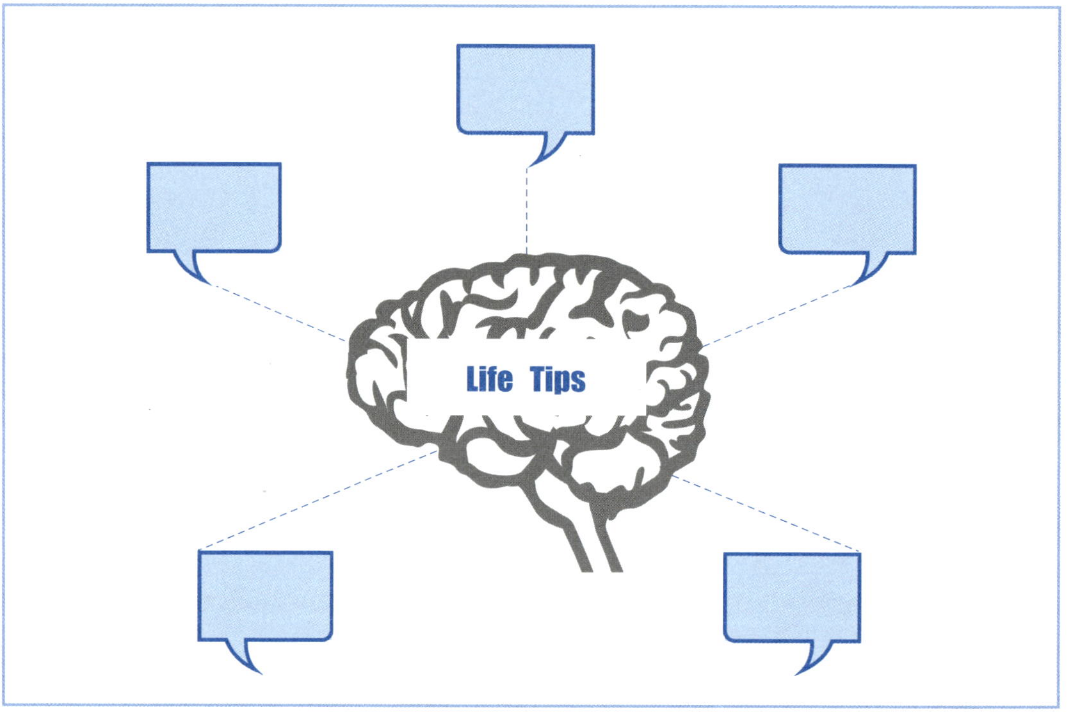

What If?

1. What if you had to teach a new student about your major? What is the number one advice you would give?

____

____

____

2. What if you could talk to anyone about your future plans? Who would you talk to and why?

____

____

____

VOCABULARY PREVIEW

1. Read and match the words or phrases with the right meaning.

a. on one's way to •	• a. strong feeling
b. badly •	• b. continue to do something
c. shyness •	• c. in the process of going or coming
d. passion •	• d. a large formal meeting
e. conference •	• e. a lack of confidence in yourself
f. self-doubt •	• f. the feeling of apprehension
g. persist •	• g. in an inadequate or unsatisfactory manner

2. Complete the sentences using the words or phrases above.

a. The most important thing for completing a project is _______________.
b. You will annoy them even more if you _______________.
c. I happened to meet my friend from high school _______________ home from school.
d. The hotel is used for exhibitions, _______________ and social events.
e. When she failed the exam, she was riddled with _______________.
f. He tried to overcome his _______________ to become an actor.
g. I don't understand why she always talks _______________ about her boss.

Eight Secrets to Success

Adapted from: Richard St. John

It all started one day on a plane, on my way to give a speech, seven years ago. A young girl from a really poor family asked me a simple little question. She said, "What leads to success?" I felt really bad, because I didn't have a good answer.

Shortly after I got off the plane, I was at a conference in a room full of successful people! I decided to ask what helped them succeed, and I just kept going. Here I am, seven years and 500 interviews later, and I'm going to tell you what really leads to success and makes successful people tick.

The first thing is passion. People who create their own success do it for love; they don't do it for money. One woman said, "I would pay someone to do what I do." And the interesting thing is: if you do it for love, the money comes anyway.

Next, is work. Australian media mogul Rupert Murdoch said to me, "It's all hard work. Nothing comes easily, but I have a lot of fun." Successful people have fun working, and they also work hard. There's no magic; it's practice, practice, practice.

The next step is focus. Canadian film director, Norman Jewison said to me, "I think it all has to do with focusing yourself on one thing." Followed by the next step; Push! David Gallo, an American designer says, "Push yourself, physically and mentally." You've got to push through shyness and self-doubt.

Step 5 is to serve! A lot of kids want to be rich, but you can't serve yourself; you've got to serve others something of value. That's the way people really get rich.

Step 6 is ideas! Bill Gates says, "I had an idea: founding the first micro-computer software company." I'd say it was a pretty good idea. And there's no magic to creativity in coming up with ideas — it's just doing some very simple things.

Next is to persist, which means never giving up. Business professional Joe Kraus says, "Persistence is the number one reason for our success." You've got to persist through failure. You've got to persist through negativity!

Finally, the last step is to pay 4,000 bucks and go to a business conference of successful people. But, if you can't do that, do the other 7 things and trust me, you'll succeed.

READING COMPREHENSION

[A] *Answer the following questions related to the article.*

1. Where did the speaker meet the poor girl?
   a. at a conference
   b. on a flight
   c. in school

2. How many interviews were completed in seven years?
   a. Five hundred
   b. Five thousand
   c. Fifty-five

3. What is the second step to success?
   a. passion
   b. focus
   c. work

4. Where is Norman Jewison from?
   a. United States
   b. Canada
   c. UK

5. What is the number one reason for success, according to Joe Kraus?
   a. Focus
   b. Ideas
   c. Peristence

[B] *Answer the questions below with a complete sentence.*

1. In your future, what would you like to be successful at?

____

2. Who is the most successful person you know? What helped them succeed?

____

[C] *Read the following statements about the article. Answer true or false.*

1. The author began six years ago. T / F
2. People who create success do it for love. T / F
3. It's impossible to work hard and have fun. T / F
4. Creativity is mostly magic. T / F
5. You've got to persist through negativity. T / F

[D] *Fill in the following summary with words from the word bank.*

Many people in the world are ❶ ____________, but most of us don't really know how to make that happen. If you were able to meet with many successful people you might learn that there are eight ❷ ____________ to success. One of those keys is money. However, if you aren't rich, there are seven other things you can do. Firstly, you should have ❸ ____________. Passion can help with the next two, which are hard work and ❹ ____________. The fourth important thing is to ❺ ____________ pushing forward. Next you should make sure you are serving others, they'll be customers after all. The most ❻ ____________ thing is to have ideas you can work with. ❼ ____________, you must persist and never give up, even when things get difficult. If you can do these things you will succeed ❽ ____________.

Word Bank

eventually	successful	passion	difficult
lastly	focus	keep	keys

GRAMMAR BUILDER (Comparisons)

Complete the following paragraphs using the words in parentheses. Change word forms if needed.

Practice 1

Some people like to live in the city, but others love to live in the country. I like to live in the city because it is ______________ (interesting) than the country. Even though the cost of living in the city is ______________ (much high) than that in the country, it is worth it. The restaurants are ______________ (good), and entertainment is ______________ (available). Store hours are ______________ (convenient), so you can go shopping any time, day or night. I enjoy walking around the city. It is true that the country is ______________ (quiet) and ______________ (clean), but city streets are ______________ (exciting). There is always something interesting. For me, the city is definitely ______________ (nice) than the country.

Practice 2

I think today has been ______________ (bad) day of my life. My car suddenly stopped in the middle of the street during rush hour this morning — ______________ (busy) time of day. I sat in the car for an hour waiting for a tow truck. ______________ (long) I sat, ______________ (nervous) I got. When I got to work, I was exhausted. This was the day we were closing ______________ (big) deal of the year. My boss called me many times about the letter I was typing. And ______________ (frequent) he called, ______________ (bad) I typed. Today was one of ______________ (hard) days of my life.

FOLLOW-UP ACTIVITY

Look at the menu. Then complete the sentences using comparatives, superlatives, and equatives.

Menu

* Broccoli with Garlic Sauce	$6.15
Beef with Broccoli	$7.85
* Beef with Dried Red Pepper	$7.95
Chicken with Broccoli	$7.15
* Chicken with Orange Sauce	$7.15

Sweet and Sour Shrimp	$9.25
Steamed Mixed Vegetables (no sugar, salt, or oil)	$4.50

* HOT AND SPICY

For example : The chicken with broccoli is more expensive that the broccoli with garlic sauce.
(The chicken with broccoli가 the broccoli with garlic sauce보다 비싸다.)

1. The sweet and sour shrimp ______________________________.
(The sweet and sour shrimp가 모든 메뉴 중 가장 비싸다.)

2. The beef with dried red pepper ______________________________.
(The beef with dried red pepper는 the sweet and sour shrimp보다 짜다.)

3. The chicken with broccoli ______________________________.
(The chicken with broccoli는 The beef with broccoli보다 싸다.)

4. The chicken with orange sauce ______________________________.
(The chicken with orange sauce는 The beef with dried red pepper만큼 맵다.)

5. The steamed mixed vegetables ______________________________.
(The steamed mixed vegetables가 가장 건강식이다.)

6. The chicken with broccoli ______________________________.
(The chicken with broccoli는 The chicken with orange sauce보다 덜 맵다.)

LIFE IS INTERESTING

Incredible Coincidences

Saved by the clouds

August 9, 1945 was a turning point in the history of the world. It was also a cloudy day in Kokura, Japan. Kokura was the site of a large factory that made bullets and bombs during World War II. Due to the clouds, American pilots couldn't see the factory, so they moved on to Nagasaki where the skies were clear, and dropped a nuclear bomb.

Change in direction

In 1905 the Academy of Fine Arts in Vienna, Austria, rejected a student; twice. The student had moved to Vienna to study art, but when his mother died he was stuck there and forced to live in a poor neighborhood. During this time he grew to hate the Jewish people and, unable to study art, he joined the German army and quickly moved through the ranks. This student's name was Adolf Hitler.

Presidential oddity

John F. Kennedy and Abraham Lincoln, both past American presidents have several interesting things in common. Lincoln's secretary was named Kennedy and Kennedy's secretary was named Lincoln. Both men were shot in the head on a Friday and were replaced by a man named Johnson. Lincoln was shot in a theater named Ford. Kennedy was shot in a Lincoln Town Car made by the Ford company.

Q1. What is the strangest thing that ever happened to you?

____

Q2. Do you believe in fate and destiny? Why or why not?

____

UNIT 08

Remember to Say Thank You

What Do You Think?

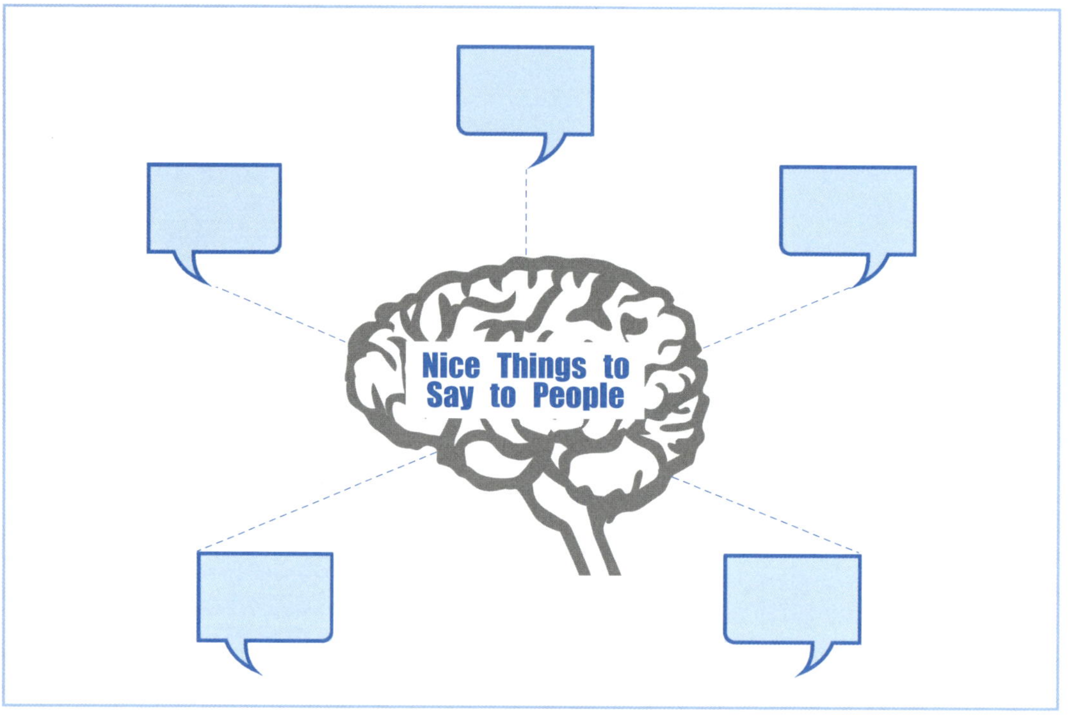

What If?

1. What if everyone could only say nice things to each other? How would the world change?

____

____

____

2. What if you could only say one nice thing per day? What would you say and to whom?

____

____

____

VOCABULARY PREVIEW

1. Read and match the words or phrases with the right meaning.

a. genuine •	• a. find out and examine to obtain the truth
b. admiration •	• b. small routine task
c. investigate •	• c. real, authentic
d. rehabilitation •	• d. being unable to stop doing something
e. addiction •	• e. expression of approval or admiration
f. chore •	• f. not secure or safe
g. insecure •	• g. restoring to a normal life by retraining

2. Complete the sentences using the words or phrases above.

a. He was ______________ due to the allegations that he stole money.

b. I'm so tired. Please help me house ______________.

c. I wanted to express my ______________ for your courage.

d. ______________ to computer games is a serious problem in our society.

e. Would you please tell me where the ______________ center is in this area?

f. If everyone starts to laugh when you walk by, it can make you feel ______________.

g. Is this painting a ______________ Picasso?

Remember to Say Thank You

Adapted from: Laura Trice

Sometimes saying nice things to others can be difficult, but why is it so hard for us to say nice things? Praise, admiration and saying thank you are important, but only when they are specific and genuine. I noticed that I would want to say thank you to someone, or say something positive, and I'd just stop. I felt shy and embarrassed, and I wondered if I was the only one. So, I decided to investigate.

I work in a rehabilitation facility, and I get to see people who are facing life and death with addiction. Sometimes the situation is simple and their core injury is easy to understand. For example, a girl's father died without saying he's proud of her. Later, she hears from family that her father told everybody else that he was proud of his daughter. The father never told her because he didn't know she needed to hear it.

After seeing countless situations like this, I wondered, why don't we ask for the things that we need? I know a married man who wants his wife to say "Thank you for working, so I can stay home with the kids," but he won't ask. If he were to ask, he would be getting something he needs, and his wife would be doing something kind for him. Hearing nice things can be powerful. For example, a friend of mine thanks her children for doing their chores. She said, "Why wouldn't I thank them, even though they're supposed to do it?"

There are people who can say kind things easily, but I wasn't one of them. So I wondered why I blocked this behavior, and why did others?

I can easily say that I would like to have steak for dinner, or that I want to go to the movies. However, I couldn't say, "Would you please praise me in this way?" The reason is that asking for praise is telling people that we are insecure. If we say that we need help, we can become scared by what others can do with this information. They could say no and neglect us, or they could abuse us. However, maybe we could actually have our needs met.

The challenge then, is to be honest about the nice things that you need to hear. Think about the things that you need to hear, but also, think about the people in your life and what they need to hear. It is okay to ask those questions so that we can help the people around us and give them a chance to help us in return. Let's make happiness a priority in our own lives, and in other's lives.

READING COMPREHENSION

[A] *Answer the following questions related to the article.*

1. What is one reason to avoid saying nice things to someone?

a. Embarrassment

b. Happiness

c. Loneliness

2. In the rehabilitation clinic, why was the girl upset about her father?

a. He was always yelling.

b. He left when she was little.

c. He didn't tell her he was proud.

3. What does it mean to ask someone to say nice things about us?

a. We're friendly

b. We're insecure

c. We're upset

4. When are praise and admiration important?

a. When we give them to people we love

b. When they're specific and genuine

c. When you hear them from your parents.

5. What should become a priority in our lives?

a. money

b. praise

c. happiness

[B] *Answer the questions below with a complete sentence.*

1. In your life, who is the most kind to you? How does it make you feel?

____

2. Are you kind to other people? Give an example.

____

[C] *Read the following statements about the article. Answer true or false.*

1. Saying nice things can be difficult. T / F
2. People are never shy about saying nice things. T / F
3. Sometimes an addict's core injury is simple. T / F
4. Saying that we need help can be scary. T / F
5. Happiness should be a priority in our lives. T / F

[D] *Fill in the following summary with words from the word bank.*

Saying kind words to other people can be ❶ ____________ for some of us. It's not that we're bad people; it's that we're sometimes ❷ ____________ or embarrassed. ❸ ____________, some people are scared to tell others about their feelings or that they need to hear nice things occasionally. For example, a husband who is ❹ ____________ telling his wife he needs to be praised. Telling others that we need to hear nice things can be scary because it shows those people that we are ❺ ____________ about ourselves. We sometimes ❻ ____________ that people will use this information to hurt us or to be ❼ ____________. However, the opposite is more likely to be true. We need to learn to ask for what we need and be unafraid to tell others positive things that can ❽ ____________ their lives.

Word Bank

unsure	difficult	worry	shy
improve	uncomfortable	unkind	furthermore

GRAMMAR BUILDER (Conjunctions/Prepositions)

Complete the paragraphs with words from the list. Use each word only once.

from, according to, than, to, not only, while, during, because, due to, compared to, but also, until, for, in, when, although

Practice 1

The state exam to become a civil servant is very popular in Korea, not only among college students and graduates, ________________ older people with work experience. There are many reasons for the high popularity such as job security and pension benefits. ________________ employees at private companies start to retire ________________ their 40s, civil servants are able to work ________________ the age of 60. The pension for public workers also gives more benefits ________________ private-sector ones ________________ the yearly payments for starting level servants are smaller than those of private companies.

Practice 2

The number of babies born prematurely or with a low birth weight is on the rise, a government study showed Tuesday. Such babies face higher health risks such as pneumonia and respiratory distress syndrome ________________ weakened immune systems or underdeveloped organs. "The number is increasing ________________ women are marrying and getting pregnant later ________________ the past" an official of the insurance agency said. ________________ the study, the number of such high-risk babies was 18,871 in 2014, accounting for 4.7 percent of the total newborns. The number has been steadily increasing, as it was 16,177 in 2010, 17,142 in 2011, 18,663 in 2012 and 18,140 in 2013. The ratio also rose from 3.8 percent to 4.4 percent ________________ the same period.

FOLLOW-UP ACTIVITY

Combine the following pairs of sentences using the prepositions and conjunctions in parentheses.

For example : You can't walk on campus late at night. You have to worry about your safety.
➜ You can't walk on campus late at night without worrying about your safety. (without)
(너의 안전에 관한 걱정 없이)

1. Students are angry with some professors. Some professors come late to class.
➜ Students are angry with some professors ______________. (because of)
(수업에 늦게 들어오시기 때문에)
➜ Students are angry with some professors ________________. (because)
(수업에 늦게 들어오시기 때문에)

2. I got an F in English conversation. I studied hard.
➜ I got an F in English conversation ____________________. (in spite of)
(열심히 공부했지만)
➜ I got an F in English conversation __________________. (even though)
(열심히 공부했지만)

3. You can get an A in English conversation next semester. You study harder.
➜ You can get an A in English conversation next semester __________. (if)
(더 열심히 공부한다면)
➜ You can't get an A in English conversation next semester _______. (unless)
(더 열심히 공부하지 않는다면)

4. He has been working at the hospital for two years. He is a doctor.
➜ He has been working at the hospital for two years ____________. (as)
(의사로서)
➜ He has been working at the hospital for two years ____________. (since)
(의사가 된 이래로)

LIFE IS INTERESTING

Health Myths

Don't eat too late at night

Many people believe that eating too late at night makes you fat, because you are inactive or sleeping. However, according to a recent study, the evening may be the best time to eat. Scientists found that those who ate their carbs in the evening, rather than during the day, were less hungry and lost more weight.

Taking a long time to stretch is helpful

Static stretching is moving one way or another and holding that position until we feel the "burn." We have learned that this is necessary to improve our workouts and prevent injury. Studies are showing that static stretching can actually slow down sprinters, make weight lifters weaker and it doesn't reduce your odds of getting hurt. Dynamic stretching is superior.

Eat low-fat foods to lose weight

"You are what you eat" is a popular saying. Some people believe that eating fat will make them fatter. Does eating more sugar make you sweeter, or more tomatoes make your skin red? Not likely. Research shows that people who eat low-fat foods tend to eat 30% more when they think the food is low fat. However, low-fat does not equal low-calorie. No matter what diet advice exists in the world, the truth is, if you eat less calories than you burn, you will lose weight.

Q1. What is a common health myth in your country that is probably not true?

____

Q2. In your opinion, what is the best way to lose weight?

____

UNIT 09

A Life Lesson from a Volunteer Firefighter

What Do You Think?

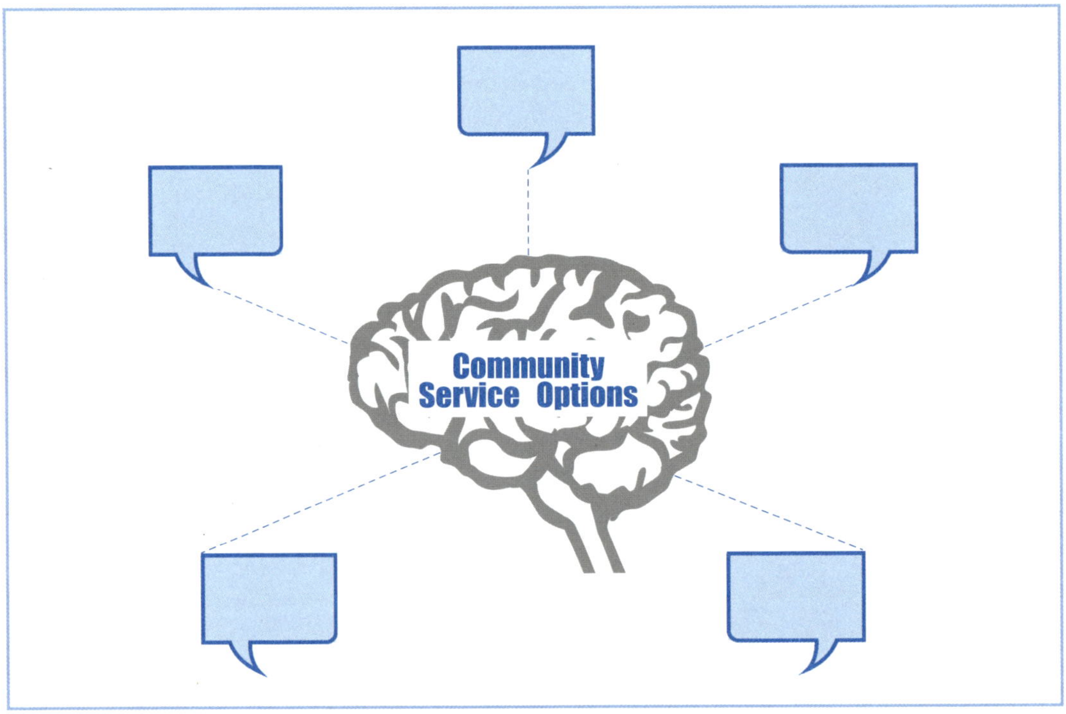

What If?

1. What if everyone had to do 10 hours of community service per week? How would our society change?

____

____

____

2. What if your home was on fire, everyone was safe, but you have time to save 1 thing? What would you save?

____

____

____

VOCABULARY PREVIEW

1. **Read and match the words or phrases with the right meaning.**

a. creature •	• a. enviousness
b. barefoot •	• b. great value
c. volunteer •	• c. an animal
d. jealousy •	• d. the quality of giving liberally
e. precious •	• e. highly valued object
f. treasure •	• f. without shoes or socks
g. generosity •	• g. person offering to do something without being compelled or paid

2. **Complete the sentences using the words or phrases above.**

a. His _______________ of his co-worker's success drove him to commit murder.

b. Diamonds are one of the most _______________ gems in the world.

c. Few _______________ came forward and helped us.

d. The family displayed great _______________ by donating a large fund to the school.

e. Most parents will tell you, the most important _______________ in their life, is their kids.

f. Night _______________ like to spend their time alone.

g. My children are running _______________ on the beach.

A Life Lesson from a Volunteer Firefighter

Adapted from: Mark Bezos

I'm from New York and I am the head of development for a non-profit organization called Robin Hood. When I'm not fighting poverty, I'm fighting fires as the assistant captain of a volunteer fire company. In our town, our volunteers help highly skilled firefighters; so we need to arrive on the fire scene early if we want to see any action.

At my very first fire, I was the second volunteer on the scene, so I had a good chance to help. However, it was still a race against the other volunteers to find the captain so we could be told what to do. When I found the captain, he was talking to the homeowner. She was clearly having one of the worst days of her life. It was the middle of the night and she was standing outside in the rain. She was under an umbrella, in her pajamas, barefoot, while her house was on fire.

One lucky volunteer got to the captain before me. He was asked to go inside and save the homeowner's dog. The dog! I was overcome with jealousy. This guy beat me by five seconds, and now he gets to tell people that he went into a burning building to save a living creature. When it was my turn the captain waved me over. He said, "Bezos, I need you to go into the house, go upstairs and get this woman a pair of shoes." This wasn't exactly what I was hoping for, but off I went.

I may have entered a burning house, but I'm no hero. I carried my precious cargo downstairs where I met my nemesis and the dog by the front door. We took our treasures to the homeowner, where his effort received much more attention than mine. A few weeks later, the fire department received a letter thanking us for our effort. In her letter, she mentioned one act of kindness before all the others: someone had gotten her a pair of shoes.

In my positions at Robin Hood and as a volunteer firefighter, I see acts of generosity and kindness on a large scale, but I also see courage on an individual basis. I've learned that all acts of kindness matter. Don't wait to make a difference in somebody's life. If you have something to give, give it now. Not every day will be a chance to save somebody's life, but every day offers us an opportunity to impact one. So get out there and save the shoes.

READING COMPREHENSION

[A] *Answer the following questions related to the article.*

1. Robin Hood is a __________.

a. firefighter

b. non-profit

c. volunteer

2. The first volunteer entered the house to __________?

a. find some shoes

b. rescue the woman

c. save the dog

3. Which acts of kindness and generosity matter the most?

a. Big ones

b. Small ones

c. All of them

4. Why was Mark jealous of the first volunteer?

a. He got to rescue the dog.

b. He was the captain's favorite.

c. He received a letter from the homeowner.

5. Every day offers us a chance to __________?

a. affect someone's life

b. be a hero

c. volunteer to help

[B] *Answer the questions below with a complete sentence.*

1. Describe a time when you helped someone.

____

2. Think of a time when someone helped you in a big way? Explain.

____

[C] *Read the following statements about the article. Answer true or false.*

1. Bezos is the captain of the fire department. T / F
2. Volunteer firefighters arrive late to help. T / F
3. The woman's house burned in the middle of the day. T / F
4. The dog received more attention than the shoes. T / F
5. If you have something to give, give it now. T / F

[D] *Fill in the following summary with words from the word bank.*

Small acts of ❶ ______________ and courage can mean a lot. When the author, Mark Bezos was volunteering as a ❷ ______________, he learned this lesson. He arrived at a fire as the second volunteer. The first ❸ ______________ was asked to rescue the homeowner's pet and Mark was asked to rescue a pair of ❹ ______________. The homeowner was surely happy to see the dog. However, in a letter to the fire ❺ ______________, the homeowner said a special thank you to the person who brought her a pair of shoes. ❻ ______________ things don't always have to be big events or items, they can be ❼ ______________ too. If you can do something kind for someone else, don't wait. Do it ❽ ______________.

Word Bank

shoes	kindness	department	today
firefighter	volunteer	small	kind

GRAMMAR BUILDER (Gerunds/Infinitives)

Complete the following paragraphs using the words in parentheses. Change verb forms if needed.

Practice 1

"________________ (raise) earned income, such as the minimum wage hike, can have a large effect on the Economic structure. The government policy should focus on this" a professor said. Others, however, say ________________ (raise) the minimum wage is not as simple in Korea compared to other countries. "Large businesses are already ________________ (pay) high salaries so they have nothing ________________ (do) with the minimum wage debate. It is small businesses that will be affected. That makes the issue more complicated" said a ________________ (rank) official at the finance ministry.

Practice 2

Can "yellow carpet" help ________________ (save) children? The International Child Rights Center (InCRC), a civic group, has continued the work of ________________ (paint) walls and pavements leading to crosswalks in school zones in yellow since April last year. They believe these "yellow carpets" will help children ________________ (avoid) car accidents.

FOLLOW-UP ACTIVITY

Read these conversations and write a summary sentence for each conversation with the verb in parentheses. Change verb forms if needed.

For example: Ann: Do you want to go swimming with me this Sunday?
Tom: No, thanks. I really don't like swimming.
Summary: Tom doesn't enjoy swimming. (enjoy)
(수영을 즐기지 않는다.)

1. Erik: Would you like to smoke?
Phil: No thanks. Due to my health, I don't smoke anymore.
Summary: Phil ______________________. (stop)
(그의 건강 때문에 담배를 끊다.)

2. Mother: Will you please do the dishes for me?
Monica: I am sorry. I have to finish the project first.
Summary: Monica ______________________. (refuse)
(그녀는 프로젝트를 끝내야 하기 때문에 설거지하는 것을 거절했다.)

3. Professor: Please come in. Make yourself comfortable.
Student: Thank you, professor.
Summary: The professor ______________________. (allow)
(학생이 들어오도록 허락했다.)

4. Ralph: Would you like to have some more cookies?
Marta: No thanks. I try to stay away from sweets.
Summary: Marta ______________________. (avoid)
(단 것 먹는 것을 피하려고 노력하다.)

5. Father: Please call me as soon as you get there.
Son: O.K.
Summary: The son ______________________. (promise)
(그의 아빠에게 전화할 것을 약속했다.)

LIFE IS INTERESTING

Populations aren't All Equal - 2015

Most populated city in the world

Shanghai is the most populous city in the world. Shanghai covers 6,340 square kilometers of coastal northeastern China. Currently, a few more than 25,000,000 people (25 million) live in Shanghai.

Nation with the highest density of people

Tiny, super rich and full of people: Monaco. Monaco is only 2.02 square kilometers. You could walk across it several times in one day. The tiny city-state has about 36,000 people. That means there are roughly 18,000 people per km^2.

The city with the highest density of people

Shanghai may have the most people, but Manila has the most human bodies squeezed into every square kilometer. Manila has 1,652,000 people, in about 38 square kilometers. That's roughly 43,000 people per km^2!

The population of the world itself

Planet Earth is a big place. Its total surface area is around 510 million square kilometers. On the surface there are around 7.1 billion people. A hundred years ago, there were about 1.6 billion and five-hundred years ago, there were around 500 million people. The population is growing rapidly, and people are heading into cities.

Q1. Do you prefer to travel in busy cities or in smaller towns? Why?

____

Q2. Do you think we should worry about the world population getting so big? Why?

____

UNIT 10

The Danger of Silence

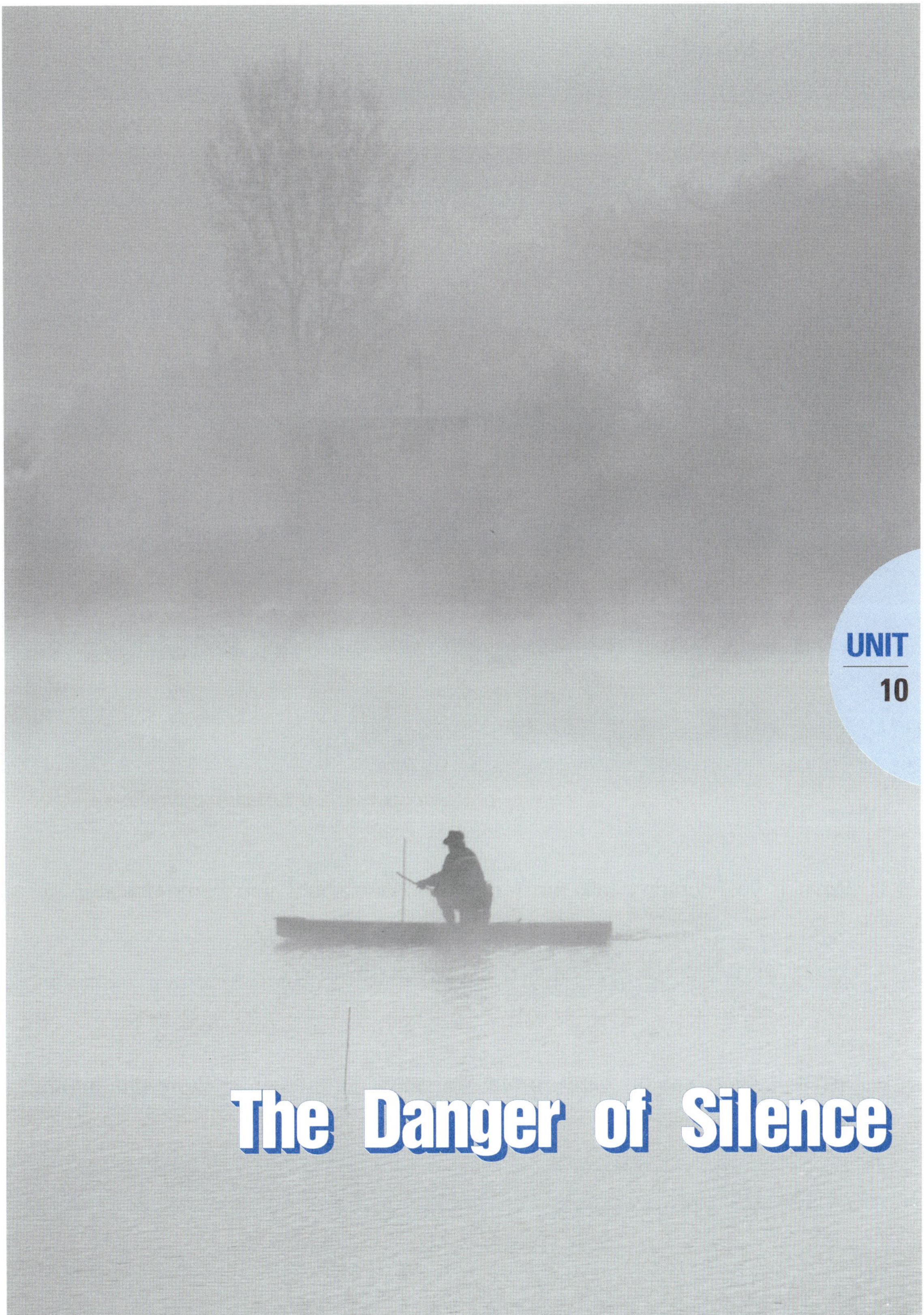

What Do You Think?

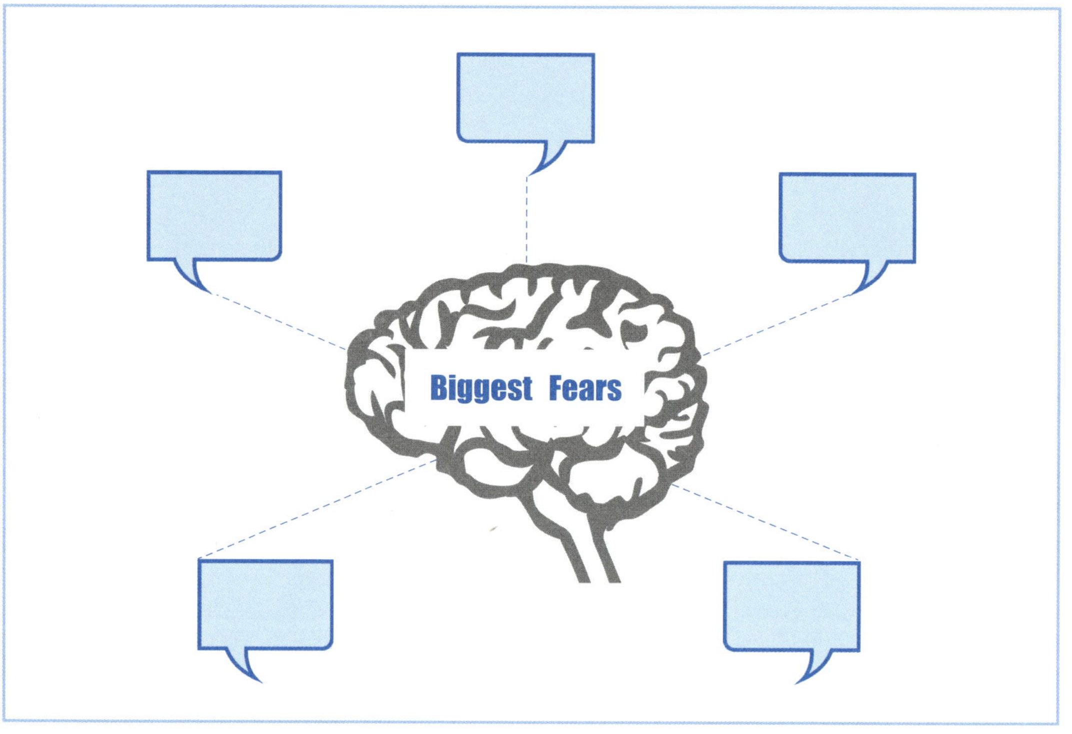

What If?

1. What if you couldn't talk for 1 month? How would you communicate?

2. What if everyone on Earth spoke the same language? How would things change?

VOCABULARY PREVIEW

1. **Read and match the words or phrases with the right meaning.**

Words	Meanings
a. discrimination •	• a. painful feeling caused by being wrong
b. violence •	• b. what remains after a part or quantity is used
c. genocide •	• c. treating a person or group differently
d. shame •	• d. think
e. figure out •	• e. lack of knowledge or information
f. ignorance •	• f. severity or harshness
g. residue •	• g. deliberate extermination of a nation or race of people

2. **Complete the sentences using the words or phrases above.**

a. It's such a ______________ that she wasn't able to make it tonight.
b. The prosecutor found drug ______________ in his hair.
c. Unfortunately, this is a clear case of indirect racial ______________.
d. I'm trying to ______________ a way that we can increase our sales.
e. I'm very depressed as my boss is in complete ______________ of my ideas for the new project.
f. We know some dictators in the world who were committing ______________.
g. The use of ______________ against anyone is a crime.

The Danger of Silence

Adapted from: Clint Smith

In 1968, Dr. Martin Luther King, Jr. was giving a speech wherein he reflects upon the Civil Rights Movement. During the speech Dr. King said, "In the end, we will remember not the words of our enemies but the silence of our friends."

Every day and everywhere we see the consequences of silence. We see things like discrimination, war, violence, and genocide. My students and I work together to fill the silences, to recognize them, to name them, and to learn that they don't have to be sources of shame.

In an effort to create a classroom where students feel safe to share their own silence, I have four rules in the front of my class. Every student learns these rules at the beginning of the year: read critically, write consciously, speak clearly, and tell your truth.

Long ago, I realized that if I was going to ask my students to speak up, I needed to tell my truth. Also, I needed to be honest with them about the times where I failed to speak up about something.

I often share a story with my students. I'm from a Catholic family and during Lent, when Catholics are asked to give up something, I always thought that the most meaningful thing I could do was sacrifice something to make God happy. I've given up soda, French fries, French kisses, and everything in between. However, one year, I gave up speaking. I figured the most valuable thing I could sacrifice was my own voice. What I didn't realize was that I had given up my voice a long time ago.

I spent so much of my life telling people the things they wanted to hear instead of the things they needed to. I told myself it wasn't my role to tell others what to do. So sometimes I wouldn't say anything; and I was accidentally encouraging other's ignorance with my silence.

We spend so much time listening to the things people are saying that we rarely pay attention to the things they don't. Silence is the residue of fear. I will not let silence wrap itself around my indecision. So this year, instead of giving something up, I will live every day as if there were a microphone tucked under my tongue. Because, you truly don't need an invitation to speak out, when all you've ever needed is your voice.

READING COMPREHENSION

[A] *Answer the following questions related to the article.*

1. What is the main idea of this speech?

a. Silence can cause big problems.

b. People talk too much.

c. Silence is important in our lives.

2. "In the end···" what will we remember more than our enemies' words?

a. The pain they caused.

b. The help of our people.

c. The silence of our friends.

3. Which of the following is not one of the four class rules?

a. Speak clearly.

b. Write neatly.

c. Read critically.

4. If we are silent around others, our silence can encourage their ___________?

a. ignorance

b. laughter

c. story telling

5. Silence is the residue of ___________?

a. failure

b. fear

c. faults

[B] *Answer the questions below with a complete sentence.*

1. Describe a time when you didn't say something important, but you should have.

____

2. How can we encourage people to talk about important problems?

____

[C] *Read the following statements about the article. Answer true or false.*

1.	Dr. King's speech was in 1967.	T / F
2.	Silence doesn't have to be a source of shame.	T / F
3.	Clint is from a Jewish family.	T / F
4.	Clint gave up speaking for a Christmas gift.	T / F
5.	You always need an invitation to speak.	T / F

[D] *Fill in the following summary with words from the word bank.*

When people fail to talk about important issues, ❶ ____________ things can happen. When we ❷ ____________ the problems of others, those problems can grow and become awful things like war and ❸ ____________. Or, our ❹ ____________ can allow things like racism and hate to continue to exist in the world. In order for us all to feel confident in our speaking, we need to ❺ ____________ that we sometimes stay silent when we should speak. While silence can be bad, so can speaking in a way that is ❻ ____________. Telling people what they want to hear, instead of what they need to hear can be bad also. If we want to help the ❼ ____________, and the people around us, to change for the better we cannot be afraid to speak out. We must use our ❽ ____________ when it is necessary or we encourage other's ignorance with our silence.

Word Bank

ignore	admit	genocide	world
terrible	silence	false	voices

GRAMMAR BUILDER (Adjective Clauses)

Complete the following paragraphs using adjective pronouns or adjective adverbs.

Practice 1

The Seoul city government said Friday it will expand the number of real estate agencies ________________ can cater to foreign customers ________________ seek accommodation facilities in the capital from the present 175 to 220, to reflect a rise in demand. The "global realty agencies" ________________ are designated by the metropolitan administration are mainly located in areas ________________ there are many expatriates, in such districts as Yongsan, Gangnam, Seocho, Songpa and Mapo. Some degree of foreign language skill is required for the realtors for customer service. Currently, there are 131 real agencies ________________ English is available, 29 agencies ________________ offer Japanese and five ________________ have Chinese. Eight others use both English and Japanese, according to the city.

Practice 2

Seoul's Noryangjin Fisheries Wholesale Market facilitates a daily trade in thousands of tons of fish and fish products. There are also 680 shops ________________ attract visitors ________________ want to get a feel and taste of Seoul's urban life. The shops were supposed to move to the new building, ________________ opened in January, according to the National Federation of Fisheries Cooperatives (NFFC). But only 200 moved and the other 480 insist ________________ they want to stay ________________ they are.

FOLLOW-UP ACTIVITY

Complete the following sentences by using adjective clauses.

For example : I like to visit places which I've never been to before.
(내가 전에 가본 적이 없는 장소들)

1. I like to stay in hotels ______________________________.
(호텔의 가격이 비싸지 않은)

2. Her pronunciation ____________________ is easy to understand.
(거의 완벽한 발음)

3. I like to travel with people ____________________________.
(내가 가장 좋아하는 사람)

4. The book ________________________________ is boring.
(내가 어제 서점에서 산 책)

5. The person _________________________ is honest and kind.
(내가 회의에서 만난 사람)

6. My grandfather bought me the bicycle ____________________.
(그것의 색이 빨갛고 노란)

7. The girl ____________________________ has two brothers.
(나의 고등학교 친구인 소녀)

8. My mother ordered her meal at the restaurant ______________.
(맛있어 보이는 식당)

9. Yosemite is the national park __________________________.
(California에 위치한 국립공원)

10. The Philippines ___________________________ is wonderful.
(많은 섬으로 이루어진 필리핀)

LIFE IS INTERESTING

Brain Hacks

Keep your goals to yourself

Do you have a goal that you really want to achieve? Keep it a secret. Studies show that sharing our goals tricks our brains into feeling like we've accomplished it already. This lowers our desire to keep going.

Change the plate

Want to eat less? Use smaller bowls and plates. Our brains tend to ignore the amount of food we see and only compare it to the emptiness of our bowl or plate. You may have enough food, but if your plate is large, your mind feels cheated. Using smaller dishes can trick your brain into thinking you're eating more than you are.

Jumpstart your day

Tired in the mornings? You can energize yourself and start your day well by stretching as much as possible in bed, before you ever get up. Also, according to recent studies, telling yourself that you had a good night's sleep is almost as effective as actually getting enough sleep.

Decisions in the dark

Need to make a difficult decision but feeling emotional? Research shows that most people think more rationally, logically and objectively in the dark.

Q1. What tricks do you use to make you life better or easier?

____

Q2. Which one of these brain hacks is going to help you the most? Why?

____

How to Succeed? Get More Sleep.

What Do You Think?

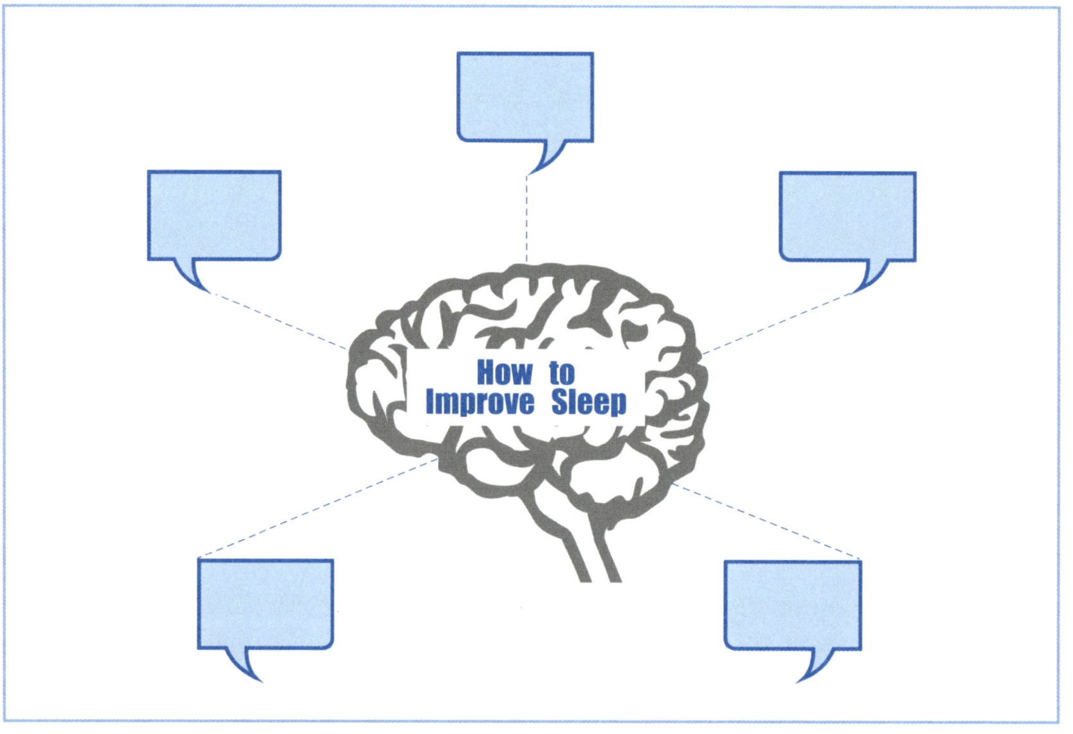

What If?

1. What if you didn't need to sleep? How would your life change?

____

____

____

2. What if you had to sleep for 8 hours every night? How would your life be different?

____

____

____

VOCABULARY PREVIEW

1. Read and match the words or phrases with the right meaning.

a. dormant •		• a. very bright
b. faint •		• b. complete or drastic change
c. revolution •		• c. lose consciousness
d. deprivation •		• d. taking something away from somebody
e. brag •		• e. temporarily inactive
f. one-upmanship •		• f. talk with too much pride
g. brilliant •		• g. art of getting the advantage over other people

2. Complete the sentences using the words or phrases above.

a. She is a scientist who is full of ______________ ideas.

b. For many people ______________ is a bad habit that annoys people around them.

c. She ______________ after she fasted for five days.

d. There are some reasons many people in modern society suffer from sleep ______________.

e. Many plants in my garden lie ______________ throughout the winter.

f. The couple has been ______________ about their new house in a big city.

g. The industrial ______________ created our modern society, but is it a good thing?

How to Succeed? Get More sleep.

Adapted from: Arianna Huffington

I recently had a big idea. It isn't a complicated idea. In fact, my big idea is a small idea that can unlock billions of other big ideas that are dormant inside us. The idea that can unlock all of those other ideas is something we take for granted every day; sleep.

I learned the value of sleep the hard way. Two-and-a-half years ago, I fainted from exhaustion. I hit my head on my desk and broke my cheekbone. I got five stitches on my right eye, and I began the journey of rediscovering the value of sleep. During this time I studied, and I met with medical doctors and scientists. From working with them, and my own experience, I'm here to tell you that the way to a more productive, inspired, and joyful life is getting enough sleep.

We women are going to lead the way in this new revolution. We are going to sleep our way to the top, literally. Unfortunately for men, sleep deprivation has become a symbol of strength. Men will brag about how little sleep they've gotten. There is this kind of sleep deprivation one-upmanship. These days in the business world, if you want to have an early meeting, and say "How about eight o'clock?" they're likely to tell you, "Eight o'clock is too late for me, but that's okay, I can play a game of tennis and do a few conference calls before I meet you at eight."

These people think it means that they are busy and productive, but the truth is they're not. At the moment, we have brilliant leaders in business and politics, making terrible decisions. Leadership is being able to see problems before they occur. However, these days the sleepy eyes of our leaders aren't able to see these issues.

As we face all the problems in our world at the moment, it's important to realize that the thing that's good for us on a personal level, the thing that will bring more joy, gratitude, and effectiveness to our lives, also happens to be what is best for the world. So I urge you to shut your eyes and discover the great ideas that lie inside us, to shut down for a while and discover the power of sleep.

READING COMPREHENSION

[A] *Answer the following questions related to the article.*

1. What can help to unlock the ideas inside of us?
   a. training
   b. sleep
   c. small ideas

2. Why did the speaker faint?
   a. She was so hungry
   b. She got very scared
   c. She was too tired

3. How much sleep is needed to be productive?
   a. A lot
   b. More than average
   c. Enough

4. For men, what has become a symbol of strength?
   a. Playing tennis in the morning.
   b. Not sleeping very much.
   c. Having many meetings.

5. Which of these things will not come into your life with more sleep?
   a. effectiveness
   b. gratitude
   c. leadership

[B] *Answer the questions below with a complete sentence.*

1. Would your life improve with more sleep? How?

____

2. What is another simple way for you to improve your life?

____

[C] *Read the following statements about the article. Answer true or false.*

1. Arianna's idea is very complicated. T / F
2. Three years ago she fainted from exhaustion. T / F
3. Arianna broke her cheekbone. T / F
4. Getting little sleep means you're busy and productive. T / F
5. These days our leaders are making all the right choices. T / F

[D] *Fill in the following summary with words from the word bank.*

Sometimes ❶ ______________ ideas can help us the most. And sometimes, it's simple things in our lives that can have the ❷ ______________ impact. Something as simple as getting enough ❸ ______________ can change our lives and help us create new ideas. Arianna Huffington learned this a few years ago when she ❹ ______________ due to exhaustion and broke her ❺ ______________. After speaking with Doctors and Scientists she concluded that sleeping enough really is a small thing that can improve our lives. Some people think sleep is ❻ ______________ and that sleeping very little means they are ❼ ______________. However, we can see that this is not always true. Getting enough sleep can help ❽ ______________ our lives and make our world a better place, one person at a time.

Word Bank

sleep	improve	productive	fainted
unimportant	cheekbone	small	greatest

GRAMMAR BUILDER (Actives/Passives)

Complete the following paragraphs using the words in parentheses. Change word forms if needed.

Practice 1

_______________ (bear) in 1927, Kim _______________ (force to) serve as a sex slave for Japanese soldiers from the age of 17. Even after the nation _______________ (liberate from) Japanese rule, she could not return to Korea and _______________ (earn) a living working at a textile factory in China. It _______________ (report) that she has been constantly hoping to return to where she _______________ (bear).

Practice 2

A patient suspected of having Middle East Respiratory Syndrome (MERS) _______________ (have/test) negative, health authorities said Wednesday. "After reviewing her blood and saliva samples, we confirmed that she _______________ (not/infect) with the disease. She _______________ (now/rest) at the National Medical Center (NMC) in central Seoul," a KCDC official said. The result came some 15 hours after the woman, whose identity _______________ (being/withhold), visited a hospital in Seoul at 2 a.m after she _______________ (suffer) from a fever, sore throat, and coughing.

FOLLOW-UP ACTIVITY

Complete the following conversation by using actives or passives.

A : ____.

(나는 어제 사고를 보았다.)

B : Oh? Where?

A : On 5th street.

B : ____?

(무슨 일이 있었는데?)

A : ______________________________________ on the street.

(motorcyclist가 트럭에 치었다.)

B : Really, ____?

(motorcyclist가 다쳤니?)

A : Yes. ________________________ and he was taken to a hospital.

(그곳에 있던 누군가가 911에 전화했다.)

________________________ in the emergency ward for cuts and bruises.

(그는 치료를 받았다.)

B : What happened to the truck driver?

A : ___________________________________ for reckless driving?

(그는 체포되었다.)

B : He's lucky that ______________________________________.

(motorcyclist가 죽지 않았다.)

LIFE IS INTERESTING

We're Changing - Part 1

Human bones

Our bones are becoming weaker. According to the National Academy of Sciences, when we changed from hunter-gatherers into farmers, around 6,000 years ago, we reduced our physical activity. This has led to a decrease in our bone mass of 20%.

Nearsightedness

More people are nearsighted now than ever before. In China, 60 years ago, only 10-20% of people were nearsighted. Now it is close to 90%. Scientists speculate that this is the result of young people spending too much time indoors.

Getting faster

Scientists measured the speed of people in over 30 cities around the world. They found that the average person walks 18.2m in about 12.5 seconds. Amazingly, this is one full second faster than 10 years ago. Scientists believe that due to long work hours and tight schedules, everyone is in more of a hurry and moving faster.

Wisdom teeth

They used to be helpful, but not so much these days. In fact, many people have them surgically removed. This is common knowledge. However, you might not know that roughly 35% of people never grow wisdom teeth. It is theorized that, in time, they'll disappear from human mouths forever.

Q1. What do you think affects people more, our DNA or our day-to-day life? Why?

____

Q2. Do you wear glasses or contact lenses? Do others in your family? Is that normal?

____

UNIT 12

Less Stuff, More Happiness

What Do You Think?

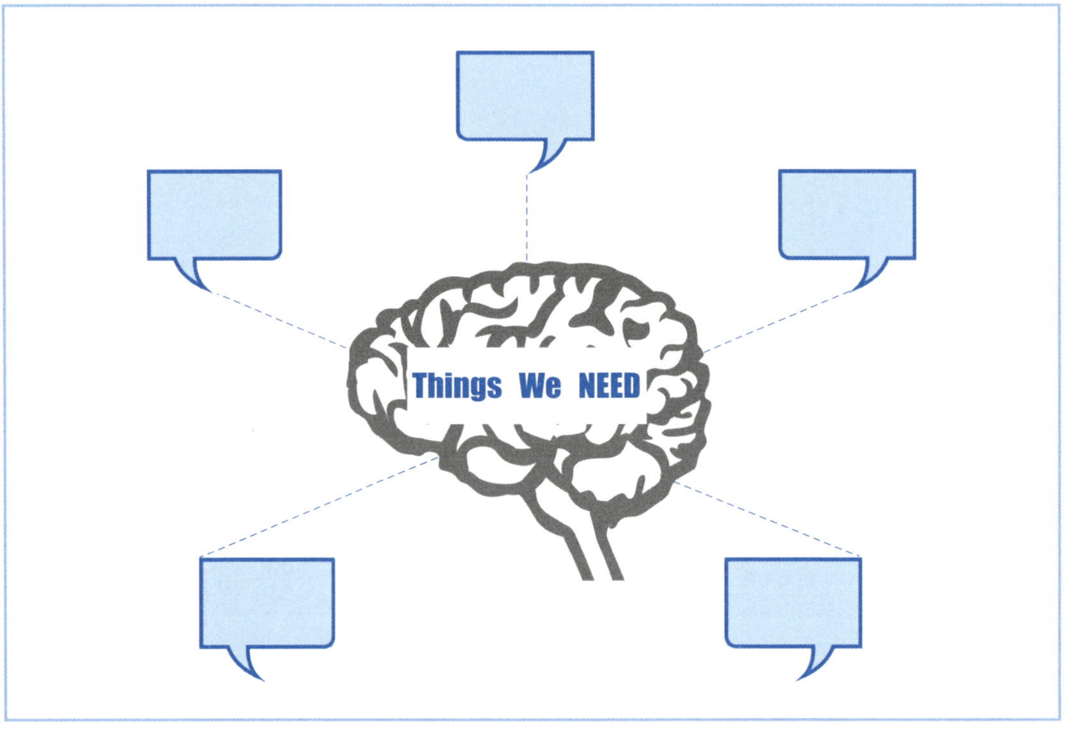

What If?

1. What if there was no more Internet? What would you do with your time?

____

____

____

2. What if you needed to fit everything you need into one suitcase? What would you bring with you?

____

____

____

VOCABULARY PREVIEW

1. Read and match the words or phrases with the right meaning.

a. plenty of •	• a. happening at the same time by chance
b. footprint •	• b. state or quality of being able to work well
c. coincidentally •	• c. mark left by a foot; area covered by something particular
d. ruthlessly •	• d. certainly
e. by all means •	• e. number or amount that is sufficient
f. efficiency •	• f. think a little
g. take a second •	• g. cruelly

2. Complete the sentences using the words or phrases above.

a. My friend and I ______________ saw each other on the street yesterday.

b. Fuel ______________ for the new model is much better than last year.

c. From the ______________ left in the snow, the person must be a man.

d. If you have any questions, ______________, feel free to ask me.

e. There are ______________ trees and flowers around the park.

f. Let's all just ______________ and calm down before we continue.

g. The dictator ______________ executed political opponents for a decade.

Less Stuff, More Happiness

Adapted from: Graham Hill

Americans have about three times the amount of space that they did 50 years ago. It's easy to think that with all the extra space, they'd have plenty of room for all that stuff. However, that's not true. In fact, there's a new industry in America, a 22 billion-dollar ($22,000,000,000) industry known as personal storage.

Americans have triple the space, but they're such good shoppers that they need even more space for all of their stuff. So where does this lead? It leads to a lot of credit card debt, huge environmental footprints, and perhaps not coincidentally, happiness levels have remained the same over the same 50 years that space has increased.

This situation is unfortunate, but there's a better way. We're finding that less might actually equal more. Many people have experienced the joys of having less: college dorm rooms, hotel rooms, camping, whatever. Among other things, this experience gave you a little more freedom, a little more time. Less stuff and less space equal a smaller footprint. It's actually a great way to also save you some money. And it will give you a little more ease in your life.

There are three main approaches to living with little. First of all, you have to edit ruthlessly. Those clothes that you haven't worn in years; it's time to let them go. We need to think before we buy and ask ourselves, "Is that really going to make me truly happier?" Certainly, if we have the money, we should buy and own great stuff. But, we want stuff that we're going to love for years, not just stuff.

Secondly, our new motto, small should be sexy. We need space efficiency. We should buy things that are designed to be used the vast majority of the time, not just some rare event. Finally, we want multifunctional spaces like a sink that is combined with a toilet, or a table that can become a bed.

We don't all need to live in $40m^2$ apartments. However, just consider the benefits of an edited life. Most of us, maybe all of us, are usually happy traveling for several days with a couple of bags and being in a small hotel room. Next time you go home and walk through the door, take a second and ask yourselves, "Could I do with a little life editing? Would that give me a little more freedom or more time?" Maybe, less does equal more. So let's make room for the good stuff, and only the good stuff.

READING COMPREHENSION

[A] *Answer the following questions related to the article.*

1. Americans have three times more space than they did __________ years ago.
   a. fifteen
   b. fifty
   c. five

2. Which of the following has not occurred due to having triple the space?
   a. credit card debt increase
   b. large environmental footprints
   c. happiness increasing

3. What can give people a smaller environmental footprint?
   a. personal storage
   b. less stuff and space
   c. recycling more often

4. Things like a sink/toilet, or a table/bed are known as __________ items.
   a. multinational
   b. multifunctional
   c. multifaceted

5. What should you do with the clothes you haven't worn in years?
   a. let them go
   b. fix them up
   c. wash them again

[B] *Answer the questions below with a complete sentence.*

1. What is something you can get rid of today, that you won't miss?

____

2. Could you benefit from having more space? Explain.

____

[C] *Read the following statements about the article. Answer true or false.*

1. Americans have 3 times the space they did 40 years ago. T / F
2. Americans are happier thanks to all their stuff. T / F
3. People have experienced joy by having less. T / F
4. We should buy things we rarely use. T / F
5. We all need to live in $40m^2$ apartments. T / F

[D] *Fill in the following summary with words from the word bank.*

Having more stuff does not ❶ ______________ that you will be happier. In fact, Americans have ❷ ______________ times more space now than they did 50 years ago, and all that space is filled with stuff. However, their level of ❸ ______________ hasn't changed. We could all benefit from living with less stuff. Many people have found ❹ ______________ and joy by using less stuff, like when they're camping or staying in a motel. To live ❺ ______________ we have to change. First, we have to edit our lives and remove the things that we don't really need. Secondly, we have to change our thinking to believe that small things are ❻ ______________. We should try to buy things that we're going to use ❼ ______________. Finally, we should have spaces in our home that can be used for more than just one thing. Living this way can give us a sense of freedom and peace that we are not getting from being surrounded by ❽ ______________. So let's make room for just the good stuff.

Word Bank

sex	stuff	often	peace
small	simply	three	guarantee

GRAMMAR BUILDER (Conditionals)

Complete the following paragraphs using the words in parentheses. Change word forms if needed.

Practice 1

If you ______________ (visit) L.A., you ______________ (find) hundreds of miles of freeways. You need to take a freeway if you ______________ (want) to go more than a few blocks in any direction. Unfortunately, when you get on a freeway, you see thousands of other individuals like you trying to drive somewhere. If you ______________ (look) around, you ______________ (notice) that most cars have only one person in them. And, if you ______________ (open) the car window, you ______________ (feel) immediately the effect of all these cars - your eyes are burned from the pollution.

Practice 2

Civil rights defend the people's rights. For Americans, civil rights are described in a part of their Constitution that is called the Bill of Rights. Some of these rights are explained below. Freedom of speech is guaranteed by the constitution. Someone speaking against the government ______________ (go to jail) if Americans ______________ (not have) this freedom. Freedom of religion is also guaranteed by the constitution. If Americans ______________ (not have) this right, it ______________ (possible) to discriminate against people because of their religious beliefs. Due process means that a person accused of a crime must receive fair treatment. If America ______________ (not have) due process, accused people ______________ (not have) any legal protection at all.

FOLLOW-UP ACTIVITY

Complete the following conversation by using the appropriate conditionals.

Mary : Didn't you go to a late-night party the night before last?

John : Yes. ______________________________ and I didn't study for my test.
(어제 큰 시험이 있었다.)
Of course, I didn't do very well on my test.
_____________________, I would have done better on it.
(시험을 위해서 열심히 공부했었다면)

Mary : Don't worry too much. That is not the only test you're going to have all semester. ______________________, ________________________.
(내가 너라면, 나는 다음 시험을 위해서 열심히 공부할 것이다.)
By the way, why did you stay so late at the party?

John : I met Jack after a long time there. Jack and I danced and talked with each other a lot.
___________________ if there hadn't been so many nice people there.
(우리는 그렇게 오랫동안 머무르지 않았을 텐데)
I wish ____.
(어제 시험을 치르지 않았기를)
________________, he probably would have let me take it at a later date.
(내가 교수님에게 요청했다면)
I hope ____ in the course.
(F를 받기 않기를)

Mary : I think you won't fail. Good luck.

John : Thanks.

We're Changing - Part 2

Learning to read and write

More and more people are becoming literate around the world. According to a UNESCO survey Eastern Europe is the region with the highest rate of literacy. According to surveys reported by the government, in North Korea, 100% of all people over the age of 15 can read and write.

Blue eyes are disappearing

Among white Americans, almost half of all people born between 1899 and 1905 had blue eyes. By 1951 this had decreased to 33%. As of the year 2006, only around 20% of all American babies had blue eyes. The stereotype of the blonde haired, blue eyed American may be disappearing.

Getting sick of being clean

We are cleaner than ever. This has reduced infectious disease deaths in the world. One side effect of this is that diseases that attack our immune system, like allergies, have increased. We need different and dirty things to make our immune system stronger. For example, exposing babies to peanuts reduces peanut allergies. In the UK, the amount of people going to the hospital for allergies increased 615% between 1992 and 2012.

Q1. What are you allergic to? How did you find out?

____

Q2. Why do you think blue eyes are disappearing in America?

____

ANSWER KEY

UNIT 01 *Speak So That People Want to Listen*

VOCABULARY PREVIEW

1. Read and match the words or phrases with the right meaning.

a. instrument (e)	a. expressing denial or refusal
b. negativity (a)	b. base; something essential
c. excuse (g)	c. genuineness
d. exaggeration (f)	d. quality of being honest and morally upright
e. cornerstone (b)	e. implement or apparatus
f. authenticity (c)	f. an overstatement
g. integrity (d)	g. providing a reason or explanation for release from an obligation

2. Complete the sentences using the words or phrases above.

a. There's a considerable exaggeration in his findings. I don't believe him.
b. Which musical instrument can you play?
c. Late again! Don't make another excuse.
d. The opposite concept of negativity is positivity.
e. The authenticity of the document could not be proven.
f. The right to privacy is a cornerstone of a democratic society.
g. He is reputed to be a man of integrity.

READING COMPREHENSION

A: 1. b 2. b 3. c 4. b 5. C

C: 1. T 2. T 3. T 4. F 5. F

D: 1. Habits 2. Badly 3. Listen 4. Item
5. Negative 6. Excuses 7. Important 8. Dogmatism

GRAMMAR BUILDER (Nouns/Articles)

Complete the following paragraphs using the words in parentheses. Change the form of the words if needed.

Practice 1

The Seoul Metropolitan Government will give an identification number to artworks
(Seoul Metropolitan Government) (identification number)
in its possession as part of its efforts to manage them better. The municipality announced on Friday that 400 of its important artworks, such as monuments and
(artwork)
statutes, will have plaques with their identification numbers, names, brief descriptions
(number)
and management bodies by the end of September. Among them, 81 artworks will be managed by art experts from the city government, while the rest of them will
(city government)
be managed by public organizations.

Practice 2

Chinese companies are a new target for Korea's tourism industry, as they offer incentive
(company)
tours for their high-performance employees. As the number of tourists reaches up
(number of)
to several thousand at once, more and more provincial governments are rolling up their sleeves to attract them. Incheon was the first this year to make headlines here
(sleeve) (first)
for attracting more than 6,000 employees of a Chinese company called Aurance in March.
(employee)

FOLLOW-UP ACTIVITY

Complete the following conversations thinking about the appropriate articles such as a, an, some, or the.

1. A : What did you do last Saturday and Sunday?

B : I saw a movie Saturday and went on a picnic with my family Sunday.
(가족과 피크닉을 갔다.)

A : Did you have fun?

B : The picnic was fun, but the movie was boring.
(영화는 지루했다.)

2. A : The fruit we bought at the store was fresh.
(우리가 그 가게에서 산 과일)

B : That's the best place to buy fruit.

3. A : I need some gas but gas is expensive nowadays.
(기름이 요즘 비싸다.)

B : The gas at this gas station is more expensive than the gas at that station.

4. A : I bought a radio. I like to listen to music when I do house chores.
(나는 음악 듣기를 좋아한다.)

B : Would you please turn the radio down? The music is too loud.
(음악이 너무 크다.)

A : No problem.

UNIT 02 *Try Something New for 30 Days*

VOCABULARY PREVIEW

1. Read and match the words or phrases with the right meaning.

a. challenge (c)	a. reach or come to a certain state
b. self-confidence (e)	b. come to understand
c. end up (a)	c. a difficult job or task
d. adventurous (f)	d. promise given by one person
e. from scratch (g)	e. having confidence in oneself
f. figure out (b)	f. full of danger and excitement
g. guarantee (d)	g. at the beginning

2. Complete the sentences using the words or phrases above.

a. Your report is terrible, start over and write it from scratch.

b. Don't worry so much. You'll be O.K. You must have more self-confidence.

c. I guarantee that he is the most talented person you've ever met.

d. Reducing the gap between poor and rich is one of the main challenges facing the government.

e. I can't figure out how the machine works.

f. If you drive so fast, you'll end up in the hospital.

g. His adventurous life in the jungle is amazing to read about.

READING COMPREHENSION

A: 1. a 2. b 3. c 4. c 5. D

C: 1. F 2. F 3. F 4. F 5. F

D: 1. Rut 2. Thirty 3. habit 4. memorable
5. badly 6. anything 7. novelist 8. do it

GRAMMAR BUILDER (Pronouns)

Complete the following paragraphs with the words from the list. Each word can be used more than once.

he, him, himself, one, another, the other, the others, they, them, I, me, it, they, myself, something, anything, nothing, anyone

Practice 1

Albert Schweitzer is one of the most famous names in the history of medicine. He decided to become a doctor when he was thirty years old. By this time, he had established himself in two other careers, music and theology. In fact, he had already published two books-one on the life of Jesus and the other on the works of Bach. Even though he became famous in these fields, he gave them up in order to become a doctor and help the sick of Africa.

Practice 2

My life is a full and happy one, and I'm grateful for all I've been given. However, I could never call my life perfect when I see so many poor, hungry, and homeless people around me. They put up with more difficulties in their lives than I will ever know, and none of it is their fault. How can my conscience not bother me? Isn't it my moral duty to help them? I feel that I'm obligated to do something and blame myself every day for doing nothing. But what one thing can I do to relieve their pain? Can anyone tell me? Can you?

FOLLOW-UP ACITIVITY

Complete the following conversations using the appropriate pronouns.

1. A : I have a book somewhere. Is this my book?
   B : No, it belongs to Tom. I think yours is over there.
   (나는 너의 것은 저기 있다고 생각한다.)
2. A : I need a red pen. Do you have one that I could borrow?
   (내가 빌릴 수 있는 것을 가지고 있나요?)
   B : No. Ask if Mary has one.
   (Mary가 가지고 있는지 물어봐.)
3. A : Where is my Korean-English dictionary? I need it.
   B : I don't know. Didn't you lend it to someone?
   (너 그것을 누군가에게 빌려주지 않았니?)
4. A : Tom has made a lot of progress in English. Last semester he couldn't order a meal in a restaurant.
   B : Yeah. His friends helped him do everything. Now he can speak English in a lot of situations.
   (그의 친구들이 그가 하는 모든 것을 도와주었다.)
5. A : I heard there was a fire in your apartment yesterday. Was anyone hurt?
   (누군가 다쳤니?)
   B : No. The firefighters got everyone out of the building.
   (소방관들이 모두를 빌딩 밖으로 내보냈다.)
6. A : Where did you get those new running shoes? They look comfortable.
   B : I found them at Sam's Sport Shop.
   (Sam's Sport Shop에서 찾았어.)

UNIT 03 *The Best Gift I Ever Survived*

VOCABULARY PREVIEW

1. Read and match the words or phrases with the right meaning.

a. incredible (c)	a. very useful
b. appreciate (f)	b. abnormal mass of new tissue
c. tumor (b)	c. impossible to believe
d. inspire (g)	d. frightening
e. motivate (e)	e. fill somebody with influence
f. valuable (a)	f. value highly
g. scary (d)	g. cause somebody to work

2. Complete the sentences using the words or phrases above.
   a. I gained some valuable experience from volunteer work.
   b. My father needs an operation to remove a tumor in his left lung.
   c. He earned an incredible amount of money after launching a startup.
   d. Watching young drivers go so fast is a little scary.
   e. His work can inspire the rest of his coworkers to do better.
   f. I really appreciate your help.
   g. The teacher always motivates his students to work harder.

READING COMPREHENSION

A: 1. c 2. b 3. b 4. b 5. C

C: 1. T 2. T 3. T 4. F 5. F

D: 1. unexpected 2. gift 3. closer 4. meet
5. lifestyle 6. appreciate 7. negative 8. positive

GRAMMAR BUILDER (Verb)

Complete the following paragraphs using the words in parentheses. Change verb forms if needed. For example, simple present, simple past, or present perfect.

Practice 1

She fell (fall) down the stairs on Feb. 15, breaking a rib that then pierced one of her lungs. She has been hospitalized (hospitalize) since the fall, but is still in serious condition. At the age of 17, she was sent (be)(send) to a military brothel in China. After Korea's liberation from Japanese occupation in 1945, she stayed (stay) in China and married (marry) a Chinese man.

Practice 2

Many modern marriages are finding interesting solutions to difficult problems. Take Mr. Kim and Ms. Lee, for example. They married (marry) in March 2012. They had lived (live) in Seoul for 2 years together before Mr. Kim moved to Pusan. In 2014 Mr. Kim got (get) a great job offer from a company in Pusan and went (go) there alone. As Ms. Lee's company is in Seoul, they have lived (live) apart ever since. They travel (travel) back and forth between Seoul and Pusan now. Sociologists call this kind of marriage a "commuter marriage". "It hasn't been easy," (not easy) says Ms. Lee. "Last month I saw (see) Mr. Kim four times, but this month I have only seen (only see) him once."

FOLLOW-UP ACTIVITY

Look at Tom's schedule and complete the sentences below.
Use a proper verb tense such as simple present, simple past, present progressive.

Tom's Schedule

17:00 a.m - 8:00 a.m get to work 8:00 a.m - 10:00 a.m check e-mails 10:00 a.m - 12:00 p.m meet and consult with my clients	12:00 p.m - 1:00 p.m have lunch 1:00 p.m - 4:00 p.m write reports and send them to the manager 4:00 p.m - 5:00 p.m return phone calls 6:00 p.m - 7:00 p.m arrive home

1. Tom usually gets to work from 7:00 a.m to 8:00 a.m.
   (Tom은 7시에서 8시 사이에 직장에 도착한다.)
2. It's 8:30 a.m At the moment, he is checking e-mails.
   (그는 지금 이메일을 확인하고 있다.)
3. It's 12:00 p.m He has been meeting and consulting with his clients since 10:00 a.m.
   (그는 10시 이후로 고객을 만나고 상담을 하고 있다.)
4. He had lunch with his co-workers at a restaurant. It's 1:30 p.m.
   (그는 그의 동료들과 식당에서 식사를 했다.)
5. He spends three hours writing reports and sending them to the manager everyday.
   (그는 매일 3시간을 보고서를 쓰고 팀장에게 보내는데 사용한다.)
6. What does he do between 4:00 p.m and 5:00 p.m?
   (4시와 5시 사이에 그는 무엇을 하나?)
7. When he met and consulted with his clients, he had already checked e-mails.
   (그가 그의 고객을 만나고 상담했을 때 그는 이미 이메일을 확인했다.)

UNIT 04 *Success is a Continuous Journey*

VOCABULARY PREVIEW

1. Read and match the words or phrases with the right meaning.

a. make it (e)	a. on the surface
b. be good at (c)	b. prevent from concentrating on something
c. come up with (g)	c. be able to perform satisfactorily
d. work at (d)	d. engage in physical or mental activity
e. pour in (f)	e. be successful in one's career

f. distract (b) f. come or go in a continuous stream

g. outwardly (a) g. find or produce

2. Complete the sentences using the words or phrases above.

a. It is too bad that he will never really make it as an actor.

b. Ms. Lee appeared outwardly calm even though she was badly surprised.

c. I find it difficult to study at home since my children distract me.

d. If you'd like to be good at a foreign language, patience and diligence are necessary.

e. My sister has been working at her project all day.

f. Every morning commuters are pouring in to the subway station.

g. He should come up with a new idea for increasing sales in China.

READING COMPREHENSION

A: 1. a 2. b 3. c 4. b 5. B

C: 1. F 2. F 3. T 4. F 5. T

D: 1. successful 2. become 3. behavior 4. depressed
5. effects 6. achieve 7. continuing 8. forward

GRAMMAR BUILDER (Subject-Verb Agreement)

Complete the following paragraphs using the words in parentheses. Change verb forms if needed.

Practice 1

Slightly more than 24 percent of households in Seoul are (be) made up of just one person. The latest figures regarding household sizes in Seoul during 2010 were (be) released in the March edition of "Seoul Economics," a monthly news letter which is (be) published by the Seoul Metropolitan Government. The figure was (be) only 4.5 percent in 1980.

The chief of the Global Future Research Center of the Seoul Institute who conducted the survey, said the rise is (be) mainly attributable to the increase in women's economic activities and the change of their views on marriage, which led to the growth of women choosing to remain single or marry at a later age.

Practice 2

Office worker Lee, 28, wishes (wish) to keep working after marriage. Such an idea has become widespread among young women over the past decade, as female participation in the workforce has grown (have grown) significantly. "In many cases young men prefer (prefer) to have their spouses work, so that both can contribute to household finances," male office worker Kim, 29, said. Figures back (back) this trend according to data from Statistics Korea, the number of women who marry (marry) without jobs or being students dropped from 169,581 in 2005 to 102,915 in 2015.

FOLLOW-UP ACTIVITY

Complete the sentences thinking about subject-verb agreement.

1. One of my friends rides a bicycle to school every day.
   (매일 학교까지 자전거를 탄다.)
2. There are important questions to be answered this morning.
   (중요한 질문들이 있다.)
3. Economics is a difficult subject to me.
   (나에게는 어려운 과목이다.)
4. The book about the American fifty states is interesting and I want to recommend it to others.
   (재미있어서 나는 다른 사람들에게 추천하고 싶다.)
5. Local news is on TV every night at 11:00 p.m.
   (매일 밤 11시에 TV에서 방송한다.)

6. Everyone is going to the movie tonight.
(오늘 밤 영화를 보러 갈 것이다.)

7. Each member of my family likes Mexican food.
(멕시코 음식을 좋아한다.)

8. The number of students in this class is twelve.
(이 수업의 학생의 수는)

9. Most of the food at the cafeteria tastes good.
(맛있다.)

10. Five thousand miles is too far to travel by car.
(너무 멀어서 차로 여행할 수 없다.)

UNIT 05 *How to Start a Movement*

VOCABUALRY PREVIEW

1. Read and match the words with the right meaning.

a. courage (c)	a. make too low an estimate
b. relatively (g)	b. cause people to laugh at
c. embrace (d)	c. ability to control fear
d. underestimate (a)	d. accept or take willingly
e. transform ~ into (e)	e. completely change
f. stand out (f)	f. be easily seen
g. make fun of (b)	g. to a particular degree, especially when compared to something similar

2. Complete the sentences using the words or phrases above.
   a. It is bad to make fun of people who are disabled.
   b. Don't underestimate others. They may be better than you.
   c. I don't have the courage to say 'no' when someone asks me to do something I don't like to do.
   d. It is time to embrace his idea and change.
   e. I woke up relatively early this morning.
   f. The yellow lettering on the sign stands out well against a dark background.
   g. We need to transform the area from a desert into a swamp.

READING COMPREHENSION

A: 1. c 2. b 3. a 4. c 5. C

C: 1. F 2. T 3. T 4. T 5. T

D: 1. movement 2. key 3. courage 4. leader
5. Eventually 6. powerful 7. change 8. follower

GRAMMAR BUILDER (Adjectives/Adverbs)

Complete the following paragraphs using the words in parentheses. Change word forms if needed.

Practice 1

Sixty-five children were killed in car accidents last year, up 25 percent from a year earlier. Nearly (near) 80 percent of the deadly (dead) accidents were reported in or near (near) crosswalks in school zones, according to police data. Children's lack of attention to approaching vehicles can be considered one reason. Another is speedy (speed) or careless (care) driving in school zones.

Practice 2

The Ministry of Health and Welfare recommended eating a variety of nutritious (nutrition) food including rice, whole grains, fruits, milk, dairy products, meat, fish, eggs and beans to ensure a balanced (balance) and healthy (health) diet. At the same time, it called on people to avoid overeating and to do more physical (physical) activities and exercise. In addition, the guidelines asked people to use more locally-grown (local) (grow) agricultural (agriculture) products.

FOLLOW-UP ACTIVITY

Complete the following letter. Each sentence should have one or more adjectives or adverbs.

Dear Mom and Dad,

Life in N.Y is very exciting, since I have never left my small hometown.
(N.Y 생활은 매우 재미있습니다.)
I was afraid of living in a big city like N.Y before coming here.
(나는 뉴욕 같은 큰 도시에 사는 것이 두려웠습니다.)
I also wasn't sure I could live without you, but I can. I love it! You'd be surprised to see me.
(나는 당신들 없이 살 수 있을지)
I walk happily down the busy street, and the noise doesn't bother me at all. There is always something to do. Yesterday, on my way home, I saw a wonderful street musician.
(나는 멋진 거리 악사를 보았습니다.)
He played the violin so beautifully.
(그는 너무 아름답게 바이올린을 연주했습니다.)
I couldn't believe he was on the street and not in a big Concert hall.
My new roommate from Korea is very kind and pretty.
(한국에서 온 새로운 룸메이트는 친절하고 예쁩니다.)
She seemed to be shy at first and hardly said anything.
(거의 어떤 것도 말하지 않았습니다.)
Now we can't stop talking and we are very good friends.
(우리는 매우 좋은 친구입니다.)
I hope you are both well. Please give my love to everyone and write back soon!
(잘 지내시길 바랍니다.)

Wendy

UNIT 06 *Got a Meeting? Take a Walk.*

VOCABULARY PREVIEW

1. Read and match the words or phrases with the right meaning.

a. generation (e) a. make somebody feel certain

b. consequence (c) — b. involving the loss or sacrifice of something
c. convince (a) — c. thing that is a result
d. bottom line (g) — d. breathe heavily
e. huff and puff (d) — e. all people born at about the same time
f. at the cost of (b) — f. keep alive
g. sustainable (f) — g. essential point

2. Complete the sentences using the words or phrases above.
   a. How can you convince me that you are innocent?.
   b. She saved her son from the fire, but at the cost of her own life.
   c. The decision you made could have serious consequences for the company.
   d. He is huffing and puffing since he ran to catch the bus.
   e. There is a generation gap between the young and the old.
   f. The bottom line is that you're just not good enough.
   g. Fresh water is less sustainable now than 40 years ago.

READING COMPREHENSION

A: 1. a 2. c 3. c 4. c 5. B

C: 1. T 2. F 3. T 4. F 5. F

D: 1. butts 2. sleep 3. cancer 4. However
5. walk 6. meetings 7. creatively 8. separately

GRAMMAR BUILDER (Participles)

Complete the following paragraphs using the words in parentheses. Change verb forms if needed.

Practice 1

A pediatrician and nutritionist at a medical center said minimizing (minimize) sugar intake from an early age is crucial in establishing (establish) and maintaining (maintain) healthy eating (eat) habits. "Once children get used to the sweetness of sugar in food, they are less likely to eat vegetables and fruits or other healthy foods that do not taste so sweet," she said. It is not good that many children and teenagers consume sugar in such large amounts.

Practice 2

The government has issued dietary guidelines in the hope of improving (improve) people's eating (eat) habits by getting (get) them to consume less salty, sweet and fatty foods and to keep a balanced (balance) diet. The measure came a day after the government declared a campaign against excessive sugar consumption, pointing out that Koreans' sugar intake has neared an alarming (alarm) level. Sugar is cited as a major cause of obesity and diabetes among Koreans.

FOLLOW-UP ACTIVITY

Complete each sentence with the participial adjective that comes from the underlined verb.

For example : The movie bored me.

→ The movie was boring and I was bored. (영화가 지루해서 나는 지루했다.)

1. The garbage in the hallway disgusted Mary.

   → The garbage was disgusting and Mary was disgusted.

   (쓰레기가 역겨워서 Mary는 역겨웠다.)

2. The subway ride exhausts Sue.

   → Sue feels exhausted because the subway ride is exhausting.

   (지하철 타는 것이 피곤해서 Sue는 피곤함을 느낀다.)

3. Those appetizers in the restaurant didn't satisfy me.

➜ As the appetizers were not satisfying, I was not satisfied.

(에피타이저는 만족스럽지 못해서 나는 만족하지 못했다.)

4. Tom's travel stories always amaze us.

➜ His stories are amazing so we are amazed.

(그의 이야기들은 놀라워서 우리는 놀랐다.)

5. I don't speak English well at all and my mistakes embarrassed me.

➜ I am embarrassed because of some embarrassing mistakes.

(나는 약간의 당황스러운 실수 때문에 당황했다.)

6. His lecture confused his students.

➜ Since his lecture was confusing, his students were confused.

(그의 강의는 혼란스러워서 그의 학생들은 혼란스러웠다.)

UNIT 07 *Eight Secrets to Success*

VOCABULARY PREVIEW

1. Read and match the words or phrases with the right meaning.

a. on one's way to (c)	a. strong feeling
b. badly (g)	b. continue to do something
c. shyness (f)	c. in the process of going or coming
d. passion (a)	d. a large formal meeting
e. conference (d)	e. a lack of confidence in yourself
f. self-doubt (e)	f. the feeling of apprehension
g. persist (b)	g. in an inadequate or unsatisfactory manner

2. Complete the sentences using the words or phrases above.

a. The most important thing for completing a project is passion.

b. You will annoy them even more if you persist.

c. I happened to meet my friend from high school on my way home from school.

d. The hotel is used for exhibitions, conference and social events.

e. When she failed the exam, she was riddled with self-doubt.

f. He tried to overcome his shyness to become an actor.

g. I don't understand why she always talks badly about her boss.

READING COMPREHENSION

A: 1. b 2. a 3. c 4. b 5. C

C: 1. F 2. T 3. F 4. F 5. T

D: 1. successful 2. keys 3. passion 4. focus 5. keep 6. difficult 7. Lastly 8. Eventually

GRAMMAR BUILDER (Comparisons)

Complete the following paragraphs using the words in parentheses. Change word forms if needed.

Practice **1**

Some people like to live in the city, but others love to live in the country. I like to live in the city because it is more interesting (interesting) than the country. Even though the cost of living in the city is much higher (much high) than that in the country, it is worth it. The restaurants are better (good), and entertainment is more available (available). Store hours are more convenient (convenient), so you can go shopping any time, day or night. I also enjoy walking around the city. It is true that the country is quieter (quiet) and cleaner (clean), but city streets are more exciting (exciting). There is always something interesting. For me, the city is definitely nicer than (nice) the country.

Practice 2

I think today has been the worst day of my life. My car suddenly stopped in the
(bad)
middle of the street during rush hour this morning – the busiest time of day. I sat
(busy)
in the car for an hour waiting for a tow truck. The longer I sat, the more nervous
(long) (nervous)
I got. When I got to work, I was exhausted. This was the day we were closing the biggest
(big)
deal of the year. My boss called me many times about the letter I was typing. And the more frequently he called, the worse I typed. Today was one of the hardest
(frequent) (bad) (hard)
days of my life.

FOLLOW-UP ACTIVITY

Look at the menu. Then complete the sentences using comparatives, superlatives, and equatives.

* Broccoli with Garlic Sauce	$6.15
Beef with Broccoli	$7.85
* Beef with Dried Red Pepper	$7.95
Chicken with Broccol	$7.15
* Chicken with Orange Sauce	$7.15

Sweet and Sour Shrimp	$9.25
Steamed Mixed Vegetables (no sugar, salt, or oil)	$4.50

* HOT AND SPICY

For example : The chicken with broccoli is more expensive than the broccoli with garlic sauce.
(The chicken with broccoli가 the broccoli with garlic sauce보다 비싸다.)

1. The sweet and sour shrimp is the most expensive of all.
(The sweet and sour shrimp가 모든 메뉴 중 가장 비싸다.)
2. The beef with dried red pepper is saltier than the sweet and sour shrimp.
(The beef with dried red pepper는 the sweet and sour shrimp보다 짜다.)
3. The chicken with broccoli is cheaper than the beef with broccoli.
(The chicken with broccoli는 The beef with broccoli보다 싸다.)

4. The chicken with orange sauce is as spicy as the beef with dried red pepper.
(The chicken with orange sauce는 The beef with dried red pepper만큼 맵다.)

5. The steamed mixed vegetables is the most healthy food.
(The steamed mixed vegetables가 가장 건강식이다.)

6. The chicken with broccoli is less spicy than the chicken with orange sauce.
(The chicken with broccoli는 The chicken with orange sauce보다 덜 맵다.)

UNIT 08 *Remember to Say Thank You*

VOCABULARY PREVIEW

1. Read and match the words or phrases with the right meaning.

a. genuine (c)	a. find out and examine to obtain the truth
b. admiration (e)	b. small routine task
c. investigate (a)	c. real, authentic
d. rehabilitation (g)	d. being unable to stop doing
e. addiction (d)	e. expression of approval or admiration
f. chore (b)	f. not secure or safe
g. insecure (f)	g. restoring to a normal life by retraining

2. Complete the sentences using the words or phrases above.
   a. He was investigated due to the allegations that he stole money.
   b. I'm so tired. Please help me house chores.
   c. I wanted to express my admiration for your courage.
   d. Addiction to computer games is a serious problem in our society.
   e. Would you please tell me where the rehabilitation centre is in this area?
   f. If everyone starts to laugh when you walk nearby, it can make you feel insecure.
   g. Is this painting a genuine Picasso?

READING COMPREHENSION

A: 1. a 2. c 3. b 4. b 5. C

C: 1. T 2. F 3. T 4. T 5. T

D: 1. difficult 2. shy 3. Further 4. uncomfortable
5. insecure 6. worry 7. unkind 8. Improve

GRAMMAR BUILDER (Conjunctions/Prepositions)

Complete the paragraphs with words from the list. Use each word only once.

from, according to, than, to, not only, while, during, because, due to, compared to, but also, until, for, in, when, although

Practice 1

The state exam to become a civil servant is very popular in Korea, not only among college students and graduates, but also older people with work experience. There are many reasons for the high popularity: job security and pension benefits. While employees at private companies start to retire in their 40s, civil servants are able to work until the age of 60. The pension for public workers also gives more benefits than private-sector ones although the yearly payments for starting level servants are smaller than those of private companies.

Practice 2

The number of babies born prematurely or with a low birth weight is on the rise, a government study showed Tuesday. Such babies face higher health risks such as pneumonia and respiratory distress syndrome due to weakened immune systems or underdeveloped organs. "The number is increasing because women are marrying and getting pregnant later compared to the past" an official of the insurance agency said. According to the study, the number of such high-risk babies was 18.871 in 2014, accounting for 4.7 percent of the total newborns. The number has been steadily increasing, as it was 16,177 in 2010, 17,142 in 2011, 18,663 in 2012 and 18,140 in 2013. The ratio also rose from 3.8 percent to 4.4 percent during the same period.

FOLLOW-UP ACTIVITY

Combine the following pairs of sentences using the prepositions and conjunctions in parentheses.

For example :

You can't walk on campus late at night. You have to worry about your safety.

➜ You can't walk on campus late at night without worrying about your safety. (without)

(너의 안전에 관한 걱정 없이)

1. Students are angry with some professors. Some professors come late to class.

➜ Students are angry with some professors because of coming late to class. (because of)

(수업에 늦게 들어오시기 때문에)

➜ Students are angry with some professors because they come late to class. (because)

(수업에 늦게 들어오시기 때문에)

2. I got an F in English conversation. I studied hard.

➜ I got an F in English conversation in spite of studying hard. (in spite of)

(열심히 공부했지만)

➜ I got an F in English conversation even though I studied hard. (even though)

(열심히 공부했지만)

3. You can get an A in English conversation next semester. You study harder.

➜ You can get an A in English conversation next semester if you study harder. (if)

(더 열심히 공부한다면)

➜ You can't get an A in English conversation next semester unless you study harder. (unless)

(만약에 더 열심히 공부하지 않으면)

4. He has been working at the hospital for two years. He is a doctor.

➜ He has been working at the hospital for two years as a doctor. (as)

(의사로서)

➜ He has been working at the hospital for two years since he became a doctor. (since)

(의사가 된 이래로)

UNIT 09 *A Life Lesson from a Volunteer Firefighter*

VOCABULARY PREVIEW

1. Read and match the words or phrases with the right meaning.

a. creature (c)	a. enviousness
b. barefoot (f)	b. great value
c. volunteer (g)	c. an animal
d. jealousy (a)	d. the quality of giving liberally
e. precious (b)	e. highly valued object
f. treasure (e)	f. without shoes or socks
g. generosity (d)	g. person offering to do something without being compelled or paid

2. Complete the sentences using the words or phrases above.

a. His jealousy of his co-worker's success drove him to commit murder.

b. Diamond is one of the most precious gems in the world.

c. Few volunteers came forward and helped us.

d. The family displayed great generosity by donating a large fund to the school.

e. Most parents will tell you, the most important treasure in their life, is their kids.

f. Night creatures like to spend their time alone.

g. My children are running barefoot on the beach.

READING COMPREHENSION

A: 1. b 2. c 3. c 4. a 5. A

C: 1. F 2. F 3. F 4. T 5. T

D: 1. kindness 2. firefighter 3. volunteer 4. shoes 5. department 6. Kind 7. small 8. today

GRAMMAR BUILDER (Gerunds/Infinitives)

Complete the following paragraphs using the words in parentheses. Change verb forms if needed.

Practice **1**

"Raising earned income, such as the minimum wage hike, can have a large effect on
(raise)
the Economic structure. The government policy should focus on this" a professor said. Others, however, say raising the minimum wage is not as simple in Korea compared
(raise)
to other countries. "Large businesses are already paying high salaries and thus they
(pay)
have nothing to do with the minimum wage debate. It is small businesses that will
(do)
be affected. That makes the issue more complicated" said a ranking official at the
(rank)
finance ministry.

Practice **2**

Can "yellow carpet" help to save children? The International Child rights Center (InCRC),
(save)
a civic group, has continued the work of painting walls and pavements leading to
(paint)
crosswalks in school zones in yellow since April last year. They believe these "yellow carpets" will help children avoid car accidents.
(avoid)

FOLLOW-UP ACTIVITY

Read these conversations and write a summary sentence for each conversation with the verb in parentheses. Change verb forms if needed.

For example : Ann : Do you want to go swimming with me this Sunday?
Tom : No, thanks. I really don't like swimming.
Summary : Tom doesn't enjoy swimming.
(enjoy)

1. Erik: Would you like to smoke?

Phil: No thanks. I don't smoke anymore due to my health.

Summary: Phil stopped smoking due to his health.
(stop)

2. Mother: Will you please do the dishes for me.

Monica: I am sorry. I have to finish the project first.

Summary: Monica refused to do the dishes because she had to finish the project.
(refuse)

3. Professor: Please come in. Make yourself comfortable.

Student: Thank you, professor.

Summary: The professor allowed the student to come in.
(allow)

4. Ralph: Would you like to have some more cookies?

Marta: No thanks. I try to stay away from sweets.

Summary: Marta tries to avoid eating sweets.
(avoid)

5. Father: Please call me as soon as you get there.

Son: O.K

Summary: The son promised to call his father.
(promise)

UNIT 10 *The Danger of Silence*

VOCABULARY PREVIEW

1. Read and match the words or phrases with the right meaning.

a. discrimination (c)	a. painful feeling caused by being wrong
b. violence (f)	b. what remains after a part or quantity is used
c. genocide (g)	c. treating a person or group differently
d. shame (a)	d. think
e. figure out (d)	e. lack of knowledge or information

f. ignorance (e) | f. severity or harshness

g. residue (b) | g. deliberate extermination of a nation or race of people

2. Complete the sentences using the words or phrases above.
   a. It's such a shame that she wasn't able to make it tonight.
   b. The prosecutor found drug residue in his hair.
   c. Unfortunately, this is a clear case of indirect racial discrimination.
   d. I'm trying to figure out away that we can increase our sales.
   e. I'm very depressed as my boss is in complete ignorance of my ideas for the new project
   f. We know some dictators in the world who were committing genocide.
   g. The use of violence against anyone is a crime.

READING COMPREHENSION

A: 1. a 2. c 3. b 4. a 5. B

C: 1. F 2. T 3. F 4. F 5. F

D: 1. terrible 2. ignore 3. genocide 4. Silence
5. admit 6. False 7. world 8. voices

GRAMMAR BUILDER (Adjective Clauses)

Complete the following paragraphs using adjective pronouns or adjective adverbs.

Practice 1

The Seoul city government said Friday it will expand the number of real estate agencies that can cater to foreign customers who seek accommodation facilities in the capital from the present 175 to 220, to reflect a rise in demand. The "global realty agencies" which are designated by the metropolitan administration are mainly located in areas where there are many expatriates, in such districts as Yongsan, Gangnam, Seocho, Songpa and Mapo. Some degree of foreign language skill is required for the realtors for customer service. Currently, there are 131 real estate agencies where English is available, 29 agencies that offer Japanese and five that have Chinese. Eight others use both English and Japanese, according to the city.

Practice 2

Seoul's Noryangjin Fisheries Wholesale Market facilitates a daily trade in thousands of tons of fish and fish products. There are also 680 shops that attract visitors who want to get a feel and taste of Seoul's urban life. The shops were supposed to move to the new building, which opened in January, according to the National Federation of Fisheries Cooperatives (NFFC). But only 200 moved and the other 480 insist that they want to stay where they are.

FOLLOW-UP ACITIVITY

Complete the following sentences by using adjective clauses.

For example : I like to visit places which I've never been to before.
(내가 전에 가본 적이 없는)

1. I like to stay in hotels whose prices are not expensive.
(가격이 비싸지 않은)
2. Her pronunciation which is almost perfect is easy to understand.
(거의 완벽한)
3. I like to travel with people whom I like the most.
(내가 가장 좋아하는)
4. The book which I bought at a book store yesterday is boring.
(내가 어제 서점에서 산)
5. The person whom I met yesterday at the conference is honest and kind.
(내가 회의에서 만난)
6. My grandfather bought me the bicycle whose color is red and yellow.
(그것의 색이 빨갛고 노란)
7. The girl who is my friend from high school has two brothers.
(나의 고등학교 친구)
8. My mother ordered her meal at the restaurant which looks good.
(맛있어 보이는)
9. Yosemite is a national park which is located in California.
(California에 위치한)

10. The Philippines, which is made of many islands, is wonderful.
(많은 섬으로 이루어진)

UNIT 11 *How to Succeed? Get More Sleep.*

VOCABULARY PREVIEW

1. Read and match the words or phrases with the right meaning.

a. dormant (e)	a. very bright
b. faint (c)	b. art of getting the advantage over other people
c. revolution (g)	c. lose consciousness
d. deprivation (d)	d. taking something away from somebody
e. brag (f)	e. temporarily inactive
f. one-upmanship (b)	f. talk with too much pride
g. brilliant (a)	g. complete or drastic change

2. Complete the sentences using the words or phrases above.
   a. She is a scientist who is full of brilliant ideas.
   b. For many people, one-upmanship is a bad habit that annoys people around them.
   c. She fainted after she fasted for five days.
   d. There are some reasons many people in modern society suffer from sleep deprivation.
   e. Many plants in my garden lie dormant throughout the winter.
   f. The couple has been bragging about their new house in a big city.
   g. The industrial revolution created our modern society, but is it a good thing?

READING COMPREHENSION

A: 1. b 2. c 3. c 4. b 5. C

C: 1. F 2. F 3. T 4. F 5. F

D: 1. small 2. greatest 3. sleep 4. fainted
5. cheekbone 6. unimportant 7. productive 8. improve

GRAMMAR BUILDER (Actives/Passives)

Complete the following paragraphs using the words in parentheses. Change word forms if needed.

Practice 1

Born (bear) in 1927, Kim was forced to (force to) serve as a sex slave for Japanese soldiers from the age of 17. Even after the nation was liberated from (liberate from) Japanese rule, she could not return to Korea and earned (earn) a living working at a textile factory in China. It is reported (report) that she has been constantly hoping to return to where she was born (bear).

Practice 2

A patient suspected of having Middle East Respiratory Syndrome (MERS) has tested (have/test) negative, health authorities said Wednesday. "After reviewing her blood and saliva samples, we confirmed that she is not infected (not/infect) with the disease. She is now resting (now/rest) at the National Medical Center (NMC) in central Seoul," A KCDC official said. The result came some 15 hours after the woman, whose identity is being withheld (being/withhold), visited a hospital in Seoul at 2 a.m after she suffered (suffer) from a fever, sore throat, and coughing.

FOLLOW-UP ACTIVITY

Complete the following conversation by using actives or passives.

A: I saw an accident yesterday.
(나는 어제 사고를 보았다.)

B: Oh? Where?

A: On the 5th street.

B: What happened?
(무슨 일이 있었는데)

A: A motorcyclist was hit by a truck on the street.
(motorcyclist가 트럭에 치었다.)

B: Really, was the motorcyclist injured?
(motorcyclist가 다쳤니?)

A: Yes. Someone there called 911 and he was taken to a hospital.
(그곳에 있던 누군가가 911에 전화했다.)
He was treated in the emergency ward for cuts and bruises.
(그는 치료를 받았다.)

B: What happened to the truck driver?

A: He was arrested for reckless driving?
(그는 체포되었다.)

B: He's lucky that the motorcyclist was not killed.
(motorcyclist가 죽지 않았다.)

UNIT 12 *Less Stuff, More Happiness*

VOCABULARY PREVIEW

1. Read and match the words or phrases with the right meaning.

a. plenty of (e)	a. happening at the same time by chance
b. footprint (c)	b. state or quality of being able to work well
c. coincidentally (a)	c. mark left by a foot
d. ruthlessly (g)	d. certainly
e. by all means (d)	e. number or amount that is sufficient
f. efficiency (b)	f. think a little
g. take a second (f)	g. cruelly

2. Complete the sentences using the words or phrases above.
a. My friend and I coincidentally saw each other on the street yesterday.
b. Fuel efficiency for the new model is much better than last year.

c. From the footprint left in the snow, the person must be a man.
d. If you have any questions, by all means, feel free to ask me.
e. There are plenty of trees and flowers around the park.
f. Let's all just take a second and calm down before we continue.
g. The dictator ruthlessly executed political opponents for a decade.

READING COMPREHENSION

A: 1. b   2. c   3. b   4. b   5. A

C: 1. F   2. F   3. T   4. F   5. F

D: 1. guarantee   2. three   3. happiness   4. peace
5. simply   6. sexy   7. often   8. stuff

GRAMMAR BUILDER (Conditionals)

Complete the following paragraphs using the words in parentheses. Change word forms if needed.

Practice 1

If you visit (visit) L.A., you will find (find) hundreds of miles of freeways. You need to take a freeway if you want (want) to go more than a few blocks in any direction. Unfortunately, when you get on a freeway, you see thousands of other individuals like you-trying to drive somewhere. If you look (look) around, you will notice (notice) that most cars have only one person in them. And, if you open (open) the car window, you will feel (feel) immediately the effect of all these cars - your eyes are burned from the pollution.

Practice 2

Civil rights defend the people's rights. For Americans, civil rights are described in a part of their Constitution that is called the Bill of Rights. Some of these rights are explained below. Freedom of speech is guaranteed by the constitution. Someone speaking against the government could go to jail (go to jail) if Americans did not have (not have) this freedom. Freedom of religion is also guaranteed by the constitution. If Americans did not have (not have) this right, it would be possible (possible) to discriminate against people because of their religious beliefs. Due process means that a person accused of a crime must receive fair treatment. If America didn't have (not have) due process, accused people wouldn't have (not have) any legal protection at all.

FOLLOW-UP ACTIVITY

Complete the following conversation by using the appropriate conditionals.

Mary: Didn't you go to a late-night party the night before last?

John: Yes. I had a big exam yesterday and I didn't study for my test.
(어제 큰 시험이 있었다.)
Of course, I didn't do very well on my test.
If I had studied for the test, I would have done better on it.
(시험을 위해서 열심히 공부했었다면)

Mary: Don't worry too much. That is not the only test you're going to have all semester.
If I were you, I would study hard for my next test.
(내가 너라면, 나는 다음 시험을 위해서 열심히 공부할 것이다.)
By the way, why did you stay so late at the party?

John: I met Jack after a long time there. Jack and I danced and talked with each other a lot.
We wouldn't have stayed so long if there hadn't been so many nice people there.
(우리는 그렇게 오랫동안 머무르지 않았을 턴데)
I wish I had not taken that test yesterday.
(어제 시험을 치르지 않았기를)

If I had asked my professor, he probably would have let me take it at a later date.
(내가 교수님에게 요청했다면)

I hope I will not get an F in the course.
(F를 받기 않기를)

Mary : I think you won't fail. Good luck.

John : Thanks.

REFERENCES

Main Topics

Adapted from talks given at TED conferences around the world.

"How to speak so that people want to listen" Julian Treasure
https://www.ted.com/talks/julian_treasure_how_to_speak_so_that_people_want_to_listen?language=en

"Try something new for 30 days" Matt Cutts
https://www.ted.com/talks/matt_cutts_try_something_new_for_30_days/transcript?language=en

"The best gift I ever survived" Stacey Kramer
http://www.ted.com/talks/stacey_kramer_the_best_gift_i_ever_survived/transcript?language=en

"Success is a continuous Journey" Richard St. John
https://www.ted.com/talks/richard_st_john_success_is_a_continuous_journey/transcript?language=en

"How to start a movement" Derek Sivers
http://www.ted.com/talks/derek_sivers_how_to_start_a_movement/transcript?language=en

"Got a meeting? Take a walk." Nilofer Merchant
https://www.ted.com/talks/nilofer_merchant_got_a_meeting_take_a_walk/transcript?language=en

"8 Secrets of Success" Richard St. John
https://www.ted.com/talks/richard_st_john_s_8_secrets_of_success/transcript?language=en

"Remember to say thank you" Laura Trice
https://www.ted.com/talks/laura_trice_suggests_we_all_say_thank_you/transcript?language=en

"A life lesson from a volunteer firefighter" Mark Bezos
http://www.ted.com/talks/mark_bezos_a_life_lesson_from_a_volunteer_firefighter/transcript?language=en

"The danger or silence" Clint Smith
https://www.ted.com/talks/clint_smith_the_danger_of_silence/transcript?language=en

"How to Succeed? Get More Sleep."
https://www.ted.com/talks/arianna_huffington_how_to_succeed_get_more_sleep/transcript?l
anguage=en

"Less stuff more happiness" Graham Hill.
https://www.ted.com/talks/graham_hill_less_stuff_more_happiness/transcript?language=en
Write

Life is Interesting

Adapted from lists composed by various websites.

"Five of the scariest places on Earth" Husna Haq
http://www.bbc.com/travel/story/20160125-five-bone-chilling-destinations

"Five legendary lost cities" Steven John
http://random-facts.top5.com/the-top-5-legendary-lost-cities/

"The top 5 eye popping facts about population density" Steven John
http://random-facts.top5.com/the-top-5-eye-popping-facts-about-population-density/

"10 craziest laws from around the world" Ejaz Khan
http://www.wonderslist.com/10-craziest-laws-in-world/

"Benefits of Laughter" Damien McGinley
http://www.top5bin.com/top-5-benefits-of-laughter/

"22 ridiculous health myths you probably believe"
http://www.cracked.com/photoplasty_1876_22-health-diet-hacks-that-will-leave-you-fat-injured/

"7 ways to know its time to break up with your job" Aaron Keifets
http://www.cracked.com/blog/7-ways-to-know-its-time-to-break-up-with-your-job/

"The 20 greatest "Butterfly Effect" moments in history"
http://www.cracked.com/photoplasty_2044_a-sandwich-caused-wwi-20-real-cases-butterfly-effect/
'5 evil species of flies you don't (want to) know exist" Jonathan Wojcik
http://www.cracked.com/article_23702_flies-that-are-way-way-too-much-like-xenomorphs.html

"22 amazing ways humans have changed in recent history" Readers
http://www.cracked.com/photoplasty_2028_our-brains-are-shrinking-22-ways-human-race-changing/

"19 brain hacks that can make you better at everyday life" Readers
http://www.cracked.com/photoplasty_2002_19-ways-to-maximize-your-brains-potential/

Elaine Kirn & Darcy Jack(1990). Interactions 1. McGraw-Hill, Inc
Marjorie Fuchs & Miriam Westheimer(1994). Focus on Grammar. Addison-Wesley Publishing Company, Inc
Patricia K. Werner & Mary Mitchell Church & Lida R. Baker(1990). Interactions II. McGraw-Hill, Inc
THE KOREA TIMES. (2016). www. Koreatimes.co.kr

A New View

College English Lessons From Around The World